TABS Screener

Temperament and Atypical Behavior Scale

Early Childhood Indicators of Developmental Dysfunction

Stephen J. Bagnato, Ed.D., N.C.S.P.
John T. Neisworth, Ph.D.
John Salvia, D.Ed.
Frances M. Hunt, Ph.D.

Instructions for administering the TABS Screener:

Please refer to Chapter 3 of the **TABS Manual** for important information before administering the TABS Screener. Complete (or have rater complete) the information in Section I. Read and discuss directions for Section II with the rater, making sure that he or she understands how to respond to the items. Ask the rater to return the Screener for scoring and interpretation when he or she has completed Section II.

I. CHILD INFORMATION

Name of child: ______________________ Sex: Female ❑ Male ❑

Date of birth: ______________________ Age (in years and months): ______________

Child's address: ______________________

Name of parent or primary caregiver in household: ______________________

Relationship to child: Mother ❑ Father ❑ Other ______________________

Telephone number: ______________________ Best time to contact: ______________

List any previously identified problems or diagnoses for this child.

1. ______________________
2. ______________________
3. ______________________

1-800-638-3775 www.brookespublishing.com

II. TABS INDICATORS

The following 15 items list some of the most frequent problems in temperament and self-regulation that parents and professionals observe in young children. Read each numbered item and check *No* if the behavior is not a problem. Check *Yes* if the behavior is a problem. Return this form to the individual administering this Screener for scoring and interpretation.

Name of rater: ______________________ Date Screener completed: ____________

Relationship to child: ______________________________

	No	Yes
1. Emotions don't match what is going on	☐	☐
2. Gets angry too easily	☐	☐
3. Too easily frustrated	☐	☐
4. Has wild temper tantrums	☐	☐
5. Frequently irritable, "touchy," or fussy	☐	☐
6. Can't comfort self when upset	☐	☐
7. Doesn't pay attention to sights and sounds	☐	☐
8. Seems to look through or past people	☐	☐
9. Resists looking you in the eye	☐	☐
10. Too "grabby," impulsive	☐	☐
11. Moods and wants are too hard to figure out	☐	☐
12. Seems to be in "own world"	☐	☐
13. "Tunes out," loses contact with what is going on	☐	☐
14. Overexcited in crowded places	☐	☐
15. Wanders around without purpose	☐	☐

III. RESULTS

Add all the items marked *Yes*, and place the total in the box below labeled Raw Score. A score of 1or 2 indicates that the child may be at risk for atypical development and self-regulatory behavior. A score of 3 or more indicates that the child's temperament and self-regulatory behavior are probably atypical for his or her age. Follow-up with a complete 55-item TABS Assessment Tool is recommended for any score other than 0.

Raw Score ☐

Recommended for follow-up with TABS Assessment Tool: Yes ☐ No ☐

 ISBN-13: 978-1-55766-423-5 ISBN-10: 1-55766-423-4
Manufactured in the United States of America.

TABS Screener

Temperament and Atypical Behavior Scale

Early Childhood Indicators of Developmental Dysfunction

Stephen J. Bagnato, Ed.D., N.C.S.P.
John T. Neisworth, Ph.D.
John Salvia, D.Ed.
Frances M. Hunt, Ph.D.

Instructions for administering the TABS Screener:

Please refer to Chapter 3 of the **TABS Manual** for important information before administering the TABS Screener. Complete (or have rater complete) the information in Section I. Read and discuss directions for Section II with the rater, making sure that he or she understands how to respond to the items. Ask the rater to return the Screener for scoring and interpretation when he or she has completed Section II.

I. CHILD INFORMATION

Name of child: ______________________ Sex: Female ❑ Male ❑

Date of birth: ______________________ Age (in years and months): ______________

Child's address: ______________________

Name of parent or primary caregiver in household: ______________________

Relationship to child: Mother ❑ Father ❑ Other ______________________

Telephone number: ______________________ Best time to contact: ______________

List any previously identified problems or diagnoses for this child.

1. ______________________
2. ______________________
3. ______________________

1-800-638-3775 www.brookespublishing.com

II. TABS INDICATORS

The following 15 items list some of the most frequent problems in temperament and self-regulation that parents and professionals observe in young children. Read each numbered item and check *No* if the behavior is not a problem. Check *Yes* if the behavior is a problem. Return this form to the individual administering this Screener for scoring and interpretation.

Name of rater: ______________________ Date Screener completed: ______________

Relationship to child: ____

	No	Yes
1. Emotions don't match what is going on	☐	☐
2. Gets angry too easily	☐	☐
3. Too easily frustrated	☐	☐
4. Has wild temper tantrums	☐	☐
5. Frequently irritable, "touchy," or fussy	☐	☐
6. Can't comfort self when upset	☐	☐
7. Doesn't pay attention to sights and sounds	☐	☐
8. Seems to look through or past people	☐	☐
9. Resists looking you in the eye	☐	☐
10. Too "grabby," impulsive	☐	☐
11. Moods and wants are too hard to figure out	☐	☐
12. Seems to be in "own world"	☐	☐
13. "Tunes out," loses contact with what is going on	☐	☐
14. Overexcited in crowded places	☐	☐
15. Wanders around without purpose	☐	☐

III. RESULTS

Add all the items marked *Yes*, and place the total in the box below labeled Raw Score. A score of 1or 2 indicates that the child may be at risk for atypical development and self-regulatory behavior. A score of 3 or more indicates that the child's temperament and self-regulatory behavior are probably atypical for his or her age. Follow-up with a complete 55-item TABS Assessment Tool is recommended for any score other than 0.

Raw Score ☐

Recommended for follow-up with TABS Assessment Tool: Yes ☐ No ☐

 ISBN-13: 978-1-55766-423-5 ISBN-10: 1-55766-423-4
Manufactured in the United States of America.

TABS Screener

Temperament and Atypical Behavior Scale

Early Childhood Indicators of Developmental Dysfunction

Stephen J. Bagnato, Ed.D., N.C.S.P.
John T. Neisworth, Ph.D.
John Salvia, D.Ed.
Frances M. Hunt, Ph.D.

Instructions for administering the TABS Screener:

Please refer to Chapter 3 of the **TABS Manual** for important information before administering the TABS Screener. Complete (or have rater complete) the information in Section I. Read and discuss directions for Section II with the rater, making sure that he or she understands how to respond to the items. Ask the rater to return the Screener for scoring and interpretation when he or she has completed Section II.

I. CHILD INFORMATION

Name of child: ______________________ Sex: Female ❑ Male ❑

Date of birth: ______________________ Age (in years and months): ______________________

Child's address: ______________________

Name of parent or primary caregiver in household: ______________________

Relationship to child: Mother ❑ Father ❑ Other ______________________

Telephone number: ______________________ Best time to contact: ______________________

List any previously identified problems or diagnoses for this child.

1. ______________________
2. ______________________
3. ______________________

1-800-638-3775 www.brookespublishing.com

II. TABS INDICATORS

The following 15 items list some of the most frequent problems in temperament and self-regulation that parents and professionals observe in young children. Read each numbered item and check *No* if the behavior is not a problem. Check *Yes* if the behavior is a problem. Return this form to the individual administering this Screener for scoring and interpretation.

Name of rater: ______________________ Date Screener completed: ______________

Relationship to child: ______________________________________

	No	Yes
1. Emotions don't match what is going on	☐	☐
2. Gets angry too easily	☐	☐
3. Too easily frustrated	☐	☐
4. Has wild temper tantrums	☐	☐
5. Frequently irritable, "touchy," or fussy	☐	☐
6. Can't comfort self when upset	☐	☐
7. Doesn't pay attention to sights and sounds	☐	☐
8. Seems to look through or past people	☐	☐
9. Resists looking you in the eye	☐	☐
10. Too "grabby," impulsive	☐	☐
11. Moods and wants are too hard to figure out	☐	☐
12. Seems to be in "own world"	☐	☐
13. "Tunes out," loses contact with what is going on	☐	☐
14. Overexcited in crowded places	☐	☐
15. Wanders around without purpose	☐	☐

III. RESULTS

Add all the items marked *Yes*, and place the total in the box below labeled Raw Score. A score of 1or 2 indicates that the child may be at risk for atypical development and self-regulatory behavior. A score of 3 or more indicates that the child's temperament and self-regulatory behavior are probably atypical for his or her age. Follow-up with a complete 55-item TABS Assessment Tool is recommended for any score other than 0.

Raw Score ☐

Recommended for follow-up with TABS Assessment Tool: Yes ❑ No ❑

 ISBN-13: 978-1-55766-423-5 ISBN-10: 1-55766-423-4
Manufactured in the United States of America.

TABS Screener

Temperament and Atypical Behavior Scale

Early Childhood Indicators of Developmental Dysfunction

Stephen J. Bagnato, Ed.D., N.C.S.P. | John T. Neisworth, Ph.D.
John Salvia, D.Ed. | Frances M. Hunt, Ph.D.

Instructions for administering the TABS Screener:

Please refer to Chapter 3 of the **TABS Manual** for important information before administering the TABS Screener. Complete (or have rater complete) the information in Section I. Read and discuss directions for Section II with the rater, making sure that he or she understands how to respond to the items. Ask the rater to return the Screener for scoring and interpretation when he or she has completed Section II.

I. CHILD INFORMATION

Name of child: ______________________ Sex: Female ❑ Male ❑

Date of birth: ______________________ Age (in years and months): ______________________

Child's address: ______________________

Name of parent or primary caregiver in household: ______________________

Relationship to child: Mother ❑ Father ❑ Other ______________________

Telephone number: ______________________ Best time to contact: ______________________

List any previously identified problems or diagnoses for this child.

1. ______________________
2. ______________________
3. ______________________

1-800-638-3775 www.brookespublishing.com

II. TABS INDICATORS

The following 15 items list some of the most frequent problems in temperament and self-regulation that parents and professionals observe in young children. Read each numbered item and check *No* if the behavior is not a problem. Check *Yes* if the behavior is a problem. Return this form to the individual administering this Screener for scoring and interpretation.

Name of rater: ______________________ Date Screener completed: ______________

Relationship to child: ______________________________________

	No	Yes
1. Emotions don't match what is going on	☐	☐
2. Gets angry too easily	☐	☐
3. Too easily frustrated	☐	☐
4. Has wild temper tantrums	☐	☐
5. Frequently irritable, "touchy," or fussy	☐	☐
6. Can't comfort self when upset	☐	☐
7. Doesn't pay attention to sights and sounds	☐	☐
8. Seems to look through or past people	☐	☐
9. Resists looking you in the eye	☐	☐
10. Too "grabby," impulsive	☐	☐
11. Moods and wants are too hard to figure out	☐	☐
12. Seems to be in "own world"	☐	☐
13. "Tunes out," loses contact with what is going on	☐	☐
14. Overexcited in crowded places	☐	☐
15. Wanders around without purpose	☐	☐

III. RESULTS

Add all the items marked *Yes*, and place the total in the box below labeled Raw Score. A score of 1or 2 indicates that the child may be at risk for atypical development and self-regulatory behavior. A score of 3 or more indicates that the child's temperament and self-regulatory behavior are probably atypical for his or her age. Follow-up with a complete 55-item TABS Assessment Tool is recommended for any score other than 0.

Raw Score ☐

Recommended for follow-up with TABS Assessment Tool: Yes ☐ No ☐

 ISBN-13: 978-1-55766-423-5 ISBN-10: 1-55766-423-4
Manufactured in the United States of America.

TABS Screener

Temperament and Atypical Behavior Scale

Early Childhood Indicators of Developmental Dysfunction

Stephen J. Bagnato, Ed.D., N.C.S.P. | John T. Neisworth, Ph.D.
John Salvia, D.Ed. | Frances M. Hunt, Ph.D.

Instructions for administering the TABS Screener:

Please refer to Chapter 3 of the **TABS Manual** for important information before administering the TABS Screener. Complete (or have rater complete) the information in Section I. Read and discuss directions for Section II with the rater, making sure that he or she understands how to respond to the items. Ask the rater to return the Screener for scoring and interpretation when he or she has completed Section II.

I. CHILD INFORMATION

Name of child: ______________________ Sex: Female ❑ Male ❑

Date of birth: ______________________ Age (in years and months): ______________

Child's address: ______________________

Name of parent or primary caregiver in household: ______________________

Relationship to child: Mother ❑ Father ❑ Other ______________________

Telephone number: ______________________ Best time to contact: ______________

List any previously identified problems or diagnoses for this child.

1. ______________________
2. ______________________
3. ______________________

II. TABS INDICATORS

The following 15 items list some of the most frequent problems in temperament and self-regulation that parents and professionals observe in young children. Read each numbered item and check *No* if the behavior is not a problem. Check *Yes* if the behavior is a problem. Return this form to the individual administering this Screener for scoring and interpretation.

Name of rater: ______________________ Date Screener completed: ______________

Relationship to child: ______________________________________

	No	Yes
1. Emotions don't match what is going on	☐	☐
2. Gets angry too easily	☐	☐
3. Too easily frustrated	☐	☐
4. Has wild temper tantrums	☐	☐
5. Frequently irritable, "touchy," or fussy	☐	☐
6. Can't comfort self when upset	☐	☐
7. Doesn't pay attention to sights and sounds	☐	☐
8. Seems to look through or past people	☐	☐
9. Resists looking you in the eye	☐	☐
10. Too "grabby," impulsive	☐	☐
11. Moods and wants are too hard to figure out	☐	☐
12. Seems to be in "own world"	☐	☐
13. "Tunes out," loses contact with what is going on	☐	☐
14. Overexcited in crowded places	☐	☐
15. Wanders around without purpose	☐	☐

III. RESULTS

Add all the items marked *Yes*, and place the total in the box below labeled Raw Score. A score of 1or 2 indicates that the child may be at risk for atypical development and self-regulatory behavior. A score of 3 or more indicates that the child's temperament and self-regulatory behavior are probably atypical for his or her age. Follow-up with a complete 55-item TABS Assessment Tool is recommended for any score other than 0.

Raw Score ☐

Recommended for follow-up with TABS Assessment Tool: Yes ☐ No ☐

 ISBN-13: 978-1-55766-423-5 ISBN-10: 1-55766-423-4
Manufactured in the United States of America.

TABS Screener

Temperament and Atypical Behavior Scale

Early Childhood Indicators of Developmental Dysfunction

Stephen J. Bagnato, Ed.D., N.C.S.P. | John T. Neisworth, Ph.D.

John Salvia, D.Ed. | Frances M. Hunt, Ph.D.

Instructions for administering the TABS Screener:

Please refer to Chapter 3 of the **TABS Manual** for important information before administering the TABS Screener. Complete (or have rater complete) the information in Section I. Read and discuss directions for Section II with the rater, making sure that he or she understands how to respond to the items. Ask the rater to return the Screener for scoring and interpretation when he or she has completed Section II.

I. CHILD INFORMATION

Name of child: ______________________ Sex: Female ❑ Male ❑

Date of birth: ______________________ Age (in years and months): ______________________

Child's address: ______________________

Name of parent or primary caregiver in household: ______________________

Relationship to child: Mother ❑ Father ❑ Other ______________________

Telephone number: ______________________ Best time to contact: ______________________

List any previously identified problems or diagnoses for this child.

1. ______________________
2. ______________________
3. ______________________

1-800-638-3775 www.brookespublishing.com

II. TABS INDICATORS

The following 15 items list some of the most frequent problems in temperament and self-regulation that parents and professionals observe in young children. Read each numbered item and check *No* if the behavior is not a problem. Check *Yes* if the behavior is a problem. Return this form to the individual administering this Screener for scoring and interpretation.

Name of rater: ______________________ Date Screener completed: ______________

Relationship to child: ____

	No	Yes
1. Emotions don't match what is going on	☐	☐
2. Gets angry too easily	☐	☐
3. Too easily frustrated	☐	☐
4. Has wild temper tantrums	☐	☐
5. Frequently irritable, "touchy," or fussy	☐	☐
6. Can't comfort self when upset	☐	☐
7. Doesn't pay attention to sights and sounds	☐	☐
8. Seems to look through or past people	☐	☐
9. Resists looking you in the eye	☐	☐
10. Too "grabby," impulsive	☐	☐
11. Moods and wants are too hard to figure out	☐	☐
12. Seems to be in "own world"	☐	☐
13. "Tunes out," loses contact with what is going on	☐	☐
14. Overexcited in crowded places	☐	☐
15. Wanders around without purpose	☐	☐

III. RESULTS

Add all the items marked *Yes*, and place the total in the box below labeled Raw Score. A score of 1or 2 indicates that the child may be at risk for atypical development and self-regulatory behavior. A score of 3 or more indicates that the child's temperament and self-regulatory behavior are probably atypical for his or her age. Follow-up with a complete 55-item TABS Assessment Tool is recommended for any score other than 0.

Raw Score ☐

Recommended for follow-up with TABS Assessment Tool: Yes ❑ No ❑

 ISBN-13: 978-1-55766-423-5 ISBN-10: 1-55766-423-4
Manufactured in the United States of America.

TABS Screener

Temperament and Atypical Behavior Scale

Early Childhood Indicators of Developmental Dysfunction

Stephen J. Bagnato, Ed.D., N.C.S.P.	John T. Neisworth, Ph.D.
John Salvia, D.Ed.	Frances M. Hunt, Ph.D.

Instructions for administering the TABS Screener:

Please refer to Chapter 3 of the **TABS Manual** for important information before administering the TABS Screener. Complete (or have rater complete) the information in Section I. Read and discuss directions for Section II with the rater, making sure that he or she understands how to respond to the items. Ask the rater to return the Screener for scoring and interpretation when he or she has completed Section II.

I. CHILD INFORMATION

Name of child: ______________________ Sex: Female ❑ Male ❑

Date of birth: ______________________ Age (in years and months): ______________

Child's address: ______________________

Name of parent or primary caregiver in household: ______________________

Relationship to child: Mother ❑ Father ❑ Other ______________________

Telephone number: ______________________ Best time to contact: ______________

List any previously identified problems or diagnoses for this child.

1. ______________________
2. ______________________
3. ______________________

II. TABS INDICATORS

The following 15 items list some of the most frequent problems in temperament and self-regulation that parents and professionals observe in young children. Read each numbered item and check *No* if the behavior is not a problem. Check *Yes* if the behavior is a problem. Return this form to the individual administering this Screener for scoring and interpretation.

Name of rater: ______________________ Date Screener completed: ______________

Relationship to child: ______________________________________

	No	Yes
1. Emotions don't match what is going on	☐	☐
2. Gets angry too easily	☐	☐
3. Too easily frustrated	☐	☐
4. Has wild temper tantrums	☐	☐
5. Frequently irritable, "touchy," or fussy	☐	☐
6. Can't comfort self when upset	☐	☐
7. Doesn't pay attention to sights and sounds	☐	☐
8. Seems to look through or past people	☐	☐
9. Resists looking you in the eye	☐	☐
10. Too "grabby," impulsive	☐	☐
11. Moods and wants are too hard to figure out	☐	☐
12. Seems to be in "own world"	☐	☐
13. "Tunes out," loses contact with what is going on	☐	☐
14. Overexcited in crowded places	☐	☐
15. Wanders around without purpose	☐	☐

III. RESULTS

Add all the items marked *Yes*, and place the total in the box below labeled Raw Score. A score of 1or 2 indicates that the child may be at risk for atypical development and self-regulatory behavior. A score of 3 or more indicates that the child's temperament and self-regulatory behavior are probably atypical for his or her age. Follow-up with a complete 55-item TABS Assessment Tool is recommended for any score other than 0.

Raw Score ☐

Recommended for follow-up with TABS Assessment Tool: Yes ☐ No ☐

 ISBN-13: 978-1-55766-423-5 ISBN-10: 1-55766-423-4
Manufactured in the United States of America.

TABS Screener

Temperament and Atypical Behavior Scale

Early Childhood Indicators of Developmental Dysfunction

Stephen J. Bagnato, Ed.D., N.C.S.P.
John T. Neisworth, Ph.D.
John Salvia, D.Ed.
Frances M. Hunt, Ph.D.

Instructions for administering the TABS Screener:

Please refer to Chapter 3 of the **TABS Manual** for important information before administering the TABS Screener. Complete (or have rater complete) the information in Section I. Read and discuss directions for Section II with the rater, making sure that he or she understands how to respond to the items. Ask the rater to return the Screener for scoring and interpretation when he or she has completed Section II.

I. CHILD INFORMATION

Name of child: ______________________ Sex: Female ❑ Male ❑

Date of birth: ______________________ Age (in years and months): ______________________

Child's address: ______________________

Name of parent or primary caregiver in household: ______________________

Relationship to child: Mother ❑ Father ❑ Other ______________________

Telephone number: ______________________ Best time to contact: ______________________

List any previously identified problems or diagnoses for this child.

1. ______________________
2. ______________________
3. ______________________

1-800-638-3775 www.brookespublishing.com

II. TABS INDICATORS

The following 15 items list some of the most frequent problems in temperament and self-regulation that parents and professionals observe in young children. Read each numbered item and check *No* if the behavior is not a problem. Check *Yes* if the behavior is a problem. Return this form to the individual administering this Screener for scoring and interpretation.

Name of rater: ______________________ Date Screener completed: ______________

Relationship to child: ______________________________________

	No	Yes
1. Emotions don't match what is going on	☐	☐
2. Gets angry too easily	☐	☐
3. Too easily frustrated	☐	☐
4. Has wild temper tantrums	☐	☐
5. Frequently irritable, "touchy," or fussy	☐	☐
6. Can't comfort self when upset	☐	☐
7. Doesn't pay attention to sights and sounds	☐	☐
8. Seems to look through or past people	☐	☐
9. Resists looking you in the eye	☐	☐
10. Too "grabby," impulsive	☐	☐
11. Moods and wants are too hard to figure out	☐	☐
12. Seems to be in "own world"	☐	☐
13. "Tunes out," loses contact with what is going on	☐	☐
14. Overexcited in crowded places	☐	☐
15. Wanders around without purpose	☐	☐

III. RESULTS

Add all the items marked *Yes*, and place the total in the box below labeled Raw Score. A score of 1or 2 indicates that the child may be at risk for atypical development and self-regulatory behavior. A score of 3 or more indicates that the child's temperament and self-regulatory behavior are probably atypical for his or her age. Follow-up with a complete 55-item TABS Assessment Tool is recommended for any score other than 0.

Raw Score ☐

Recommended for follow-up with TABS Assessment Tool: Yes ☐ No ☐

 ISBN-13: 978-1-55766-423-5 ISBN-10: 1-55766-423-4
Manufactured in the United States of America.

TABS Screener

Temperament and Atypical Behavior Scale

Early Childhood Indicators of Developmental Dysfunction

Stephen J. Bagnato, Ed.D., N.C.S.P. | John T. Neisworth, Ph.D.
John Salvia, D.Ed. | Frances M. Hunt, Ph.D.

Instructions for administering the TABS Screener:

Please refer to Chapter 3 of the **TABS Manual** for important information before administering the TABS Screener. Complete (or have rater complete) the information in Section I. Read and discuss directions for Section II with the rater, making sure that he or she understands how to respond to the items. Ask the rater to return the Screener for scoring and interpretation when he or she has completed Section II.

I. CHILD INFORMATION

Name of child: ______________________ Sex: Female ❑ Male ❑

Date of birth: ______________________ Age (in years and months): ______________________

Child's address: ______________________

Name of parent or primary caregiver in household: ______________________

Relationship to child: Mother ❑ Father ❑ Other ______________________

Telephone number: ______________________ Best time to contact: ______________________

List any previously identified problems or diagnoses for this child.

1. ______________________
2. ______________________
3. ______________________

1-800-638-3775 www.brookespublishing.com

II. TABS INDICATORS

The following 15 items list some of the most frequent problems in temperament and self-regulation that parents and professionals observe in young children. Read each numbered item and check *No* if the behavior is not a problem. Check *Yes* if the behavior is a problem. Return this form to the individual administering this Screener for scoring and interpretation.

Name of rater: ______________________ Date Screener completed: ______________

Relationship to child: ______________________

	No	Yes
1. Emotions don't match what is going on	☐	☐
2. Gets angry too easily	☐	☐
3. Too easily frustrated	☐	☐
4. Has wild temper tantrums	☐	☐
5. Frequently irritable, "touchy," or fussy	☐	☐
6. Can't comfort self when upset	☐	☐
7. Doesn't pay attention to sights and sounds	☐	☐
8. Seems to look through or past people	☐	☐
9. Resists looking you in the eye	☐	☐
10. Too "grabby," impulsive	☐	☐
11. Moods and wants are too hard to figure out	☐	☐
12. Seems to be in "own world"	☐	☐
13. "Tunes out," loses contact with what is going on	☐	☐
14. Overexcited in crowded places	☐	☐
15. Wanders around without purpose	☐	☐

III. RESULTS

Add all the items marked *Yes*, and place the total in the box below labeled Raw Score. A score of 1or 2 indicates that the child may be at risk for atypical development and self-regulatory behavior. A score of 3 or more indicates that the child's temperament and self-regulatory behavior are probably atypical for his or her age. Follow-up with a complete 55-item TABS Assessment Tool is recommended for any score other than 0.

Raw Score ☐

Recommended for follow-up with TABS Assessment Tool: Yes ☐ No ☐

 ISBN-13: 978-1-55766-423-5 ISBN-10: 1-55766-423-4
Manufactured in the United States of America.

TABS Screener

Temperament and Atypical Behavior Scale

Early Childhood Indicators of Developmental Dysfunction

Stephen J. Bagnato, Ed.D., N.C.S.P.	John T. Neisworth, Ph.D.
John Salvia, D.Ed.	Frances M. Hunt, Ph.D.

Instructions for administering the TABS Screener:

Please refer to Chapter 3 of the **TABS Manual** for important information before administering the TABS Screener. Complete (or have rater complete) the information in Section I. Read and discuss directions for Section II with the rater, making sure that he or she understands how to respond to the items. Ask the rater to return the Screener for scoring and interpretation when he or she has completed Section II.

I. CHILD INFORMATION

Name of child: ______________________ Sex: Female ❑ Male ❑

Date of birth: ______________________ Age (in years and months): ______________________

Child's address: ______________________

Name of parent or primary caregiver in household: ______________________

Relationship to child: Mother ❑ Father ❑ Other ______________________

Telephone number: ______________________ Best time to contact: ______________________

List any previously identified problems or diagnoses for this child.

1. ______________________
2. ______________________
3. ______________________

II. TABS INDICATORS

The following 15 items list some of the most frequent problems in temperament and self-regulation that parents and professionals observe in young children. Read each numbered item and check *No* if the behavior is not a problem. Check *Yes* if the behavior is a problem. Return this form to the individual administering this Screener for scoring and interpretation.

Name of rater: ______________________ Date Screener completed: ____________

Relationship to child: ______________________________

	No	Yes
1. Emotions don't match what is going on	☐	☐
2. Gets angry too easily	☐	☐
3. Too easily frustrated	☐	☐
4. Has wild temper tantrums	☐	☐
5. Frequently irritable, "touchy," or fussy	☐	☐
6. Can't comfort self when upset	☐	☐
7. Doesn't pay attention to sights and sounds	☐	☐
8. Seems to look through or past people	☐	☐
9. Resists looking you in the eye	☐	☐
10. Too "grabby," impulsive	☐	☐
11. Moods and wants are too hard to figure out	☐	☐
12. Seems to be in "own world"	☐	☐
13. "Tunes out," loses contact with what is going on	☐	☐
14. Overexcited in crowded places	☐	☐
15. Wanders around without purpose	☐	☐

III. RESULTS

Add all the items marked *Yes*, and place the total in the box below labeled Raw Score. A score of 1or 2 indicates that the child may be at risk for atypical development and self-regulatory behavior. A score of 3 or more indicates that the child's temperament and self-regulatory behavior are probably atypical for his or her age. Follow-up with a complete 55-item TABS Assessment Tool is recommended for any score other than 0.

Raw Score ☐

Recommended for follow-up with TABS Assessment Tool: Yes ☐ No ☐

 ISBN-13: 978-1-55766-423-5 ISBN-10: 1-55766-423-4
Manufactured in the United States of America.

TABS Screener

Temperament and Atypical Behavior Scale

Early Childhood Indicators of Developmental Dysfunction

Stephen J. Bagnato, Ed.D., N.C.S.P.	John T. Neisworth, Ph.D.
John Salvia, D.Ed.	Frances M. Hunt, Ph.D.

Instructions for administering the TABS Screener:

Please refer to Chapter 3 of the **TABS Manual** for important information before administering the TABS Screener. Complete (or have rater complete) the information in Section I. Read and discuss directions for Section II with the rater, making sure that he or she understands how to respond to the items. Ask the rater to return the Screener for scoring and interpretation when he or she has completed Section II.

I. CHILD INFORMATION

Name of child: ____________________ Sex: Female ☐ Male ☐

Date of birth: ____________________ Age (in years and months): ____________________

Child's address: ____________________

Name of parent or primary caregiver in household: ____________________

Relationship to child: Mother ☐ Father ☐ Other ____________________

Telephone number: ____________________ Best time to contact: ____________________

List any previously identified problems or diagnoses for this child.

1. ____________________
2. ____________________
3. ____________________

1-800-638-3775 www.brookespublishing.com

II. TABS INDICATORS

The following 15 items list some of the most frequent problems in temperament and self-regulation that parents and professionals observe in young children. Read each numbered item and check *No* if the behavior is not a problem. Check *Yes* if the behavior is a problem. Return this form to the individual administering this Screener for scoring and interpretation.

Name of rater: ______________________ Date Screener completed: ____________

Relationship to child: ______________________________________

	No	Yes
1. Emotions don't match what is going on	☐	☐
2. Gets angry too easily	☐	☐
3. Too easily frustrated	☐	☐
4. Has wild temper tantrums	☐	☐
5. Frequently irritable, "touchy," or fussy	☐	☐
6. Can't comfort self when upset	☐	☐
7. Doesn't pay attention to sights and sounds	☐	☐
8. Seems to look through or past people	☐	☐
9. Resists looking you in the eye	☐	☐
10. Too "grabby," impulsive	☐	☐
11. Moods and wants are too hard to figure out	☐	☐
12. Seems to be in "own world"	☐	☐
13. "Tunes out," loses contact with what is going on	☐	☐
14. Overexcited in crowded places	☐	☐
15. Wanders around without purpose	☐	☐

III. RESULTS

Add all the items marked *Yes*, and place the total in the box below labeled Raw Score. A score of 1or 2 indicates that the child may be at risk for atypical development and self-regulatory behavior. A score of 3 or more indicates that the child's temperament and self-regulatory behavior are probably atypical for his or her age. Follow-up with a complete 55-item TABS Assessment Tool is recommended for any score other than 0.

Raw Score ☐

Recommended for follow-up with TABS Assessment Tool: Yes ❑ No ❑

 ISBN-13: 978-1-55766-423-5 ISBN-10: 1-55766-423-4
Manufactured in the United States of America.

TABS Screener

Temperament and Atypical Behavior Scale

Early Childhood Indicators of Developmental Dysfunction

Stephen J. Bagnato, Ed.D., N.C.S.P. | John T. Neisworth, Ph.D.

John Salvia, D.Ed. | Frances M. Hunt, Ph.D.

Instructions for administering the TABS Screener:

Please refer to Chapter 3 of the **TABS Manual** for important information before administering the TABS Screener. Complete (or have rater complete) the information in Section I. Read and discuss directions for Section II with the rater, making sure that he or she understands how to respond to the items. Ask the rater to return the Screener for scoring and interpretation when he or she has completed Section II.

I. CHILD INFORMATION

Name of child: ____________________ Sex: Female ❑ Male ❑

Date of birth: ____________________ Age (in years and months): ____________

Child's address: ____________________

Name of parent or primary caregiver in household: ____________________

Relationship to child: Mother ❑ Father ❑ Other ____________________

Telephone number: ____________________ Best time to contact: ____________

List any previously identified problems or diagnoses for this child.

1. ____________________
2. ____________________
3. ____________________

1-800-638-3775 www.brookespublishing.com

II. TABS INDICATORS

The following 15 items list some of the most frequent problems in temperament and self-regulation that parents and professionals observe in young children. Read each numbered item and check *No* if the behavior is not a problem. Check *Yes* if the behavior is a problem. Return this form to the individual administering this Screener for scoring and interpretation.

Name of rater: ______________________ Date Screener completed: ____________

Relationship to child: ______________________

	No	Yes
1. Emotions don't match what is going on	☐	☐
2. Gets angry too easily	☐	☐
3. Too easily frustrated	☐	☐
4. Has wild temper tantrums	☐	☐
5. Frequently irritable, "touchy," or fussy	☐	☐
6. Can't comfort self when upset	☐	☐
7. Doesn't pay attention to sights and sounds	☐	☐
8. Seems to look through or past people	☐	☐
9. Resists looking you in the eye	☐	☐
10. Too "grabby," impulsive	☐	☐
11. Moods and wants are too hard to figure out	☐	☐
12. Seems to be in "own world"	☐	☐
13. "Tunes out," loses contact with what is going on	☐	☐
14. Overexcited in crowded places	☐	☐
15. Wanders around without purpose	☐	☐

III. RESULTS

Add all the items marked *Yes*, and place the total in the box below labeled Raw Score. A score of 1or 2 indicates that the child may be at risk for atypical development and self-regulatory behavior. A score of 3 or more indicates that the child's temperament and self-regulatory behavior are probably atypical for his or her age. Follow-up with a complete 55-item TABS Assessment Tool is recommended for any score other than 0.

Raw Score ☐

Recommended for follow-up with TABS Assessment Tool: Yes ☐ No ☐

 ISBN-13: 978-1-55766-423-5 ISBN-10: 1-55766-423-4
Manufactured in the United States of America.

TABS Screener

Temperament and Atypical Behavior Scale

Early Childhood Indicators of Developmental Dysfunction

Stephen J. Bagnato, Ed.D., N.C.S.P. | John T. Neisworth, Ph.D.
John Salvia, D.Ed. | Frances M. Hunt, Ph.D.

Instructions for administering the TABS Screener:

Please refer to Chapter 3 of the **TABS Manual** for important information before administering the TABS Screener. Complete (or have rater complete) the information in Section I. Read and discuss directions for Section II with the rater, making sure that he or she understands how to respond to the items. Ask the rater to return the Screener for scoring and interpretation when he or she has completed Section II.

I. CHILD INFORMATION

Name of child: ______________________ Sex: Female ❑ Male ❑

Date of birth: ______________________ Age (in years and months): ______________________

Child's address: ______________________

Name of parent or primary caregiver in household: ______________________

Relationship to child: Mother ❑ Father ❑ Other ______________________

Telephone number: ______________________ Best time to contact: ______________________

List any previously identified problems or diagnoses for this child.

1. ______________________
2. ______________________
3. ______________________

1-800-638-3775 www.brookespublishing.com

II. TABS INDICATORS

The following 15 items list some of the most frequent problems in temperament and self-regulation that parents and professionals observe in young children. Read each numbered item and check *No* if the behavior is not a problem. Check *Yes* if the behavior is a problem. Return this form to the individual administering this Screener for scoring and interpretation.

Name of rater: ______________________ Date Screener completed: ______________

Relationship to child: ______________________

	No	Yes
1. Emotions don't match what is going on	☐	☐
2. Gets angry too easily	☐	☐
3. Too easily frustrated	☐	☐
4. Has wild temper tantrums	☐	☐
5. Frequently irritable, "touchy," or fussy	☐	☐
6. Can't comfort self when upset	☐	☐
7. Doesn't pay attention to sights and sounds	☐	☐
8. Seems to look through or past people	☐	☐
9. Resists looking you in the eye	☐	☐
10. Too "grabby," impulsive	☐	☐
11. Moods and wants are too hard to figure out	☐	☐
12. Seems to be in "own world"	☐	☐
13. "Tunes out," loses contact with what is going on	☐	☐
14. Overexcited in crowded places	☐	☐
15. Wanders around without purpose	☐	☐

III. RESULTS

Add all the items marked *Yes*, and place the total in the box below labeled Raw Score. A score of 1or 2 indicates that the child may be at risk for atypical development and self-regulatory behavior. A score of 3 or more indicates that the child's temperament and self-regulatory behavior are probably atypical for his or her age. Follow-up with a complete 55-item TABS Assessment Tool is recommended for any score other than 0.

Raw Score ☐

Recommended for follow-up with TABS Assessment Tool: Yes ☐ No ☐

 ISBN-13: 978-1-55766-423-5 ISBN-10: 1-55766-423-4
Manufactured in the United States of America.

TABS Screener

Temperament and Atypical Behavior Scale

Early Childhood Indicators of Developmental Dysfunction

Stephen J. Bagnato, Ed.D., N.C.S.P. | John T. Neisworth, Ph.D.
John Salvia, D.Ed. | Frances M. Hunt, Ph.D.

Instructions for administering the TABS Screener:

Please refer to Chapter 3 of the **TABS Manual** for important information before administering the TABS Screener. Complete (or have rater complete) the information in Section I. Read and discuss directions for Section II with the rater, making sure that he or she understands how to respond to the items. Ask the rater to return the Screener for scoring and interpretation when he or she has completed Section II.

I. CHILD INFORMATION

Name of child: ______________________ Sex: Female ❑ Male ❑

Date of birth: ______________________ Age (in years and months): ______________

Child's address: ______________________

Name of parent or primary caregiver in household: ______________________

Relationship to child: Mother ❑ Father ❑ Other ______________________

Telephone number: ______________________ Best time to contact: ______________

List any previously identified problems or diagnoses for this child.

1. ______________________
2. ______________________
3. ______________________

1-800-638-3775 www.brookespublishing.com

II. TABS INDICATORS

The following 15 items list some of the most frequent problems in temperament and self-regulation that parents and professionals observe in young children. Read each numbered item and check *No* if the behavior is not a problem. Check *Yes* if the behavior is a problem. Return this form to the individual administering this Screener for scoring and interpretation.

Name of rater: ______________________ Date Screener completed: ______________

Relationship to child: ______________________________

	No	Yes
1. Emotions don't match what is going on	☐	☐
2. Gets angry too easily	☐	☐
3. Too easily frustrated	☐	☐
4. Has wild temper tantrums	☐	☐
5. Frequently irritable, "touchy," or fussy	☐	☐
6. Can't comfort self when upset	☐	☐
7. Doesn't pay attention to sights and sounds	☐	☐
8. Seems to look through or past people	☐	☐
9. Resists looking you in the eye	☐	☐
10. Too "grabby," impulsive	☐	☐
11. Moods and wants are too hard to figure out	☐	☐
12. Seems to be in "own world"	☐	☐
13. "Tunes out," loses contact with what is going on	☐	☐
14. Overexcited in crowded places	☐	☐
15. Wanders around without purpose	☐	☐

III. RESULTS

Add all the items marked *Yes*, and place the total in the box below labeled Raw Score. A score of 1or 2 indicates that the child may be at risk for atypical development and self-regulatory behavior. A score of 3 or more indicates that the child's temperament and self-regulatory behavior are probably atypical for his or her age. Follow-up with a complete 55-item TABS Assessment Tool is recommended for any score other than 0.

Raw Score ☐

Recommended for follow-up with TABS Assessment Tool: Yes ☐ No ☐

 ISBN-13: 978-1-55766-423-5 ISBN-10: 1-55766-423-4
Manufactured in the United States of America.

TABS Screener

Temperament and Atypical Behavior Scale

Early Childhood Indicators of Developmental Dysfunction

Stephen J. Bagnato, Ed.D., N.C.S.P. | John T. Neisworth, Ph.D.

John Salvia, D.Ed. | Frances M. Hunt, Ph.D.

Instructions for administering the TABS Screener:

Please refer to Chapter 3 of the **TABS Manual** for important information before administering the TABS Screener. Complete (or have rater complete) the information in Section I. Read and discuss directions for Section II with the rater, making sure that he or she understands how to respond to the items. Ask the rater to return the Screener for scoring and interpretation when he or she has completed Section II.

I. CHILD INFORMATION

Name of child: ______________________ Sex: Female ❑ Male ❑

Date of birth: ______________________ Age (in years and months): ______________

Child's address: ______________________

Name of parent or primary caregiver in household: ______________________

Relationship to child: Mother ❑ Father ❑ Other ______________________

Telephone number: ______________________ Best time to contact: ______________

List any previously identified problems or diagnoses for this child.

1. ______________________
2. ______________________
3. ______________________

1-800-638-3775 www.brookespublishing.com

II. TABS INDICATORS

The following 15 items list some of the most frequent problems in temperament and self-regulation that parents and professionals observe in young children. Read each numbered item and check *No* if the behavior is not a problem. Check *Yes* if the behavior is a problem. Return this form to the individual administering this Screener for scoring and interpretation.

Name of rater: ______________________ Date Screener completed: ______________

Relationship to child: ______________________________

	No	Yes
1. Emotions don't match what is going on	☐	☐
2. Gets angry too easily	☐	☐
3. Too easily frustrated	☐	☐
4. Has wild temper tantrums	☐	☐
5. Frequently irritable, "touchy," or fussy	☐	☐
6. Can't comfort self when upset	☐	☐
7. Doesn't pay attention to sights and sounds	☐	☐
8. Seems to look through or past people	☐	☐
9. Resists looking you in the eye	☐	☐
10. Too "grabby," impulsive	☐	☐
11. Moods and wants are too hard to figure out	☐	☐
12. Seems to be in "own world"	☐	☐
13. "Tunes out," loses contact with what is going on	☐	☐
14. Overexcited in crowded places	☐	☐
15. Wanders around without purpose	☐	☐

III. RESULTS

Add all the items marked *Yes*, and place the total in the box below labeled Raw Score. A score of 1or 2 indicates that the child may be at risk for atypical development and self-regulatory behavior. A score of 3 or more indicates that the child's temperament and self-regulatory behavior are probably atypical for his or her age. Follow-up with a complete 55-item TABS Assessment Tool is recommended for any score other than 0.

Raw Score ☐

Recommended for follow-up with TABS Assessment Tool: Yes ❑ No ❑

 ISBN-13: 978-1-55766-423-5 ISBN-10: 1-55766-423-4
Manufactured in the United States of America.

TABS Screener

Temperament and Atypical Behavior Scale

Early Childhood Indicators of Developmental Dysfunction

Stephen J. Bagnato, Ed.D., N.C.S.P. | John T. Neisworth, Ph.D.
John Salvia, D.Ed. | Frances M. Hunt, Ph.D.

Instructions for administering the TABS Screener:

Please refer to Chapter 3 of the **TABS Manual** for important information before administering the TABS Screener. Complete (or have rater complete) the information in Section I. Read and discuss directions for Section II with the rater, making sure that he or she understands how to respond to the items. Ask the rater to return the Screener for scoring and interpretation when he or she has completed Section II.

I. CHILD INFORMATION

Name of child: ______________________ Sex: Female ❑ Male ❑

Date of birth: ______________________ Age (in years and months): ______________

Child's address: ______________________

Name of parent or primary caregiver in household: ______________________

Relationship to child: Mother ❑ Father ❑ Other ______________________

Telephone number: ______________________ Best time to contact: ______________

List any previously identified problems or diagnoses for this child.

1. ______________________
2. ______________________
3. ______________________

1-800-638-3775 www.brookespublishing.com

II. TABS INDICATORS

The following 15 items list some of the most frequent problems in temperament and self-regulation that parents and professionals observe in young children. Read each numbered item and check *No* if the behavior is not a problem. Check *Yes* if the behavior is a problem. Return this form to the individual administering this Screener for scoring and interpretation.

Name of rater: ______________________ Date Screener completed: ______________

Relationship to child: ______________________________________

	No	Yes
1. Emotions don't match what is going on	☐	☐
2. Gets angry too easily	☐	☐
3. Too easily frustrated	☐	☐
4. Has wild temper tantrums	☐	☐
5. Frequently irritable, "touchy," or fussy	☐	☐
6. Can't comfort self when upset	☐	☐
7. Doesn't pay attention to sights and sounds	☐	☐
8. Seems to look through or past people	☐	☐
9. Resists looking you in the eye	☐	☐
10. Too "grabby," impulsive	☐	☐
11. Moods and wants are too hard to figure out	☐	☐
12. Seems to be in "own world"	☐	☐
13. "Tunes out," loses contact with what is going on	☐	☐
14. Overexcited in crowded places	☐	☐
15. Wanders around without purpose	☐	☐

III. RESULTS

Add all the items marked *Yes*, and place the total in the box below labeled Raw Score. A score of 1or 2 indicates that the child may be at risk for atypical development and self-regulatory behavior. A score of 3 or more indicates that the child's temperament and self-regulatory behavior are probably atypical for his or her age. Follow-up with a complete 55-item TABS Assessment Tool is recommended for any score other than 0.

Raw Score ☐

Recommended for follow-up with TABS Assessment Tool: Yes ❑ No ❑

 ISBN-13: 978-1-55766-423-5 ISBN-10: 1-55766-423-4
Manufactured in the United States of America.

TABS Screener

Temperament and Atypical Behavior Scale

Early Childhood Indicators of Developmental Dysfunction

Stephen J. Bagnato, Ed.D., N.C.S.P. | John T. Neisworth, Ph.D.
John Salvia, D.Ed. | Frances M. Hunt, Ph.D.

Instructions for administering the TABS Screener:

Please refer to Chapter 3 of the **TABS Manual** for important information before administering the TABS Screener. Complete (or have rater complete) the information in Section I. Read and discuss directions for Section II with the rater, making sure that he or she understands how to respond to the items. Ask the rater to return the Screener for scoring and interpretation when he or she has completed Section II.

I. CHILD INFORMATION

Name of child: ______________________ Sex: Female ❑ Male ❑

Date of birth: ______________________ Age (in years and months): ______________

Child's address: ____

Name of parent or primary caregiver in household: ______________________

Relationship to child: Mother ❑ Father ❑ Other ______________________

Telephone number: ______________________ Best time to contact: ______________

List any previously identified problems or diagnoses for this child.

1. ____
2. ____
3. ____

1-800-638-3775 www.brookespublishing.com

II. TABS INDICATORS

The following 15 items list some of the most frequent problems in temperament and self-regulation that parents and professionals observe in young children. Read each numbered item and check *No* if the behavior is not a problem. Check *Yes* if the behavior is a problem. Return this form to the individual administering this Screener for scoring and interpretation.

Name of rater: ______________________ Date Screener completed: ______________

Relationship to child: ______________________________________

	No	Yes
1. Emotions don't match what is going on	☐	☐
2. Gets angry too easily	☐	☐
3. Too easily frustrated	☐	☐
4. Has wild temper tantrums	☐	☐
5. Frequently irritable, "touchy," or fussy	☐	☐
6. Can't comfort self when upset	☐	☐
7. Doesn't pay attention to sights and sounds	☐	☐
8. Seems to look through or past people	☐	☐
9. Resists looking you in the eye	☐	☐
10. Too "grabby," impulsive	☐	☐
11. Moods and wants are too hard to figure out	☐	☐
12. Seems to be in "own world"	☐	☐
13. "Tunes out," loses contact with what is going on	☐	☐
14. Overexcited in crowded places	☐	☐
15. Wanders around without purpose	☐	☐

III. RESULTS

Add all the items marked *Yes*, and place the total in the box below labeled Raw Score. A score of 1or 2 indicates that the child may be at risk for atypical development and self-regulatory behavior. A score of 3 or more indicates that the child's temperament and self-regulatory behavior are probably atypical for his or her age. Follow-up with a complete 55-item TABS Assessment Tool is recommended for any score other than 0.

Raw Score ☐

Recommended for follow-up with TABS Assessment Tool: Yes ❑ No ❑

 ISBN-13: 978-1-55766-423-5 ISBN-10: 1-55766-423-4
Manufactured in the United States of America.

TABS Screener

Temperament and Atypical Behavior Scale

Early Childhood Indicators of Developmental Dysfunction

Stephen J. Bagnato, Ed.D., N.C.S.P.	John T. Neisworth, Ph.D.
John Salvia, D.Ed.	Frances M. Hunt, Ph.D.

Instructions for administering the TABS Screener:

Please refer to Chapter 3 of the **TABS Manual** for important information before administering the TABS Screener. Complete (or have rater complete) the information in Section I. Read and discuss directions for Section II with the rater, making sure that he or she understands how to respond to the items. Ask the rater to return the Screener for scoring and interpretation when he or she has completed Section II.

I. CHILD INFORMATION

Name of child: ____________________ Sex: Female ❑ Male ❑

Date of birth: ____________________ Age (in years and months): ____________

Child's address: ____________________

Name of parent or primary caregiver in household: ____________________

Relationship to child: Mother ❑ Father ❑ Other ____________________

Telephone number: ____________________ Best time to contact: ____________

List any previously identified problems or diagnoses for this child.

1. ____________________
2. ____________________
3. ____________________

1-800-638-3775 www.brookespublishing.com

II. TABS INDICATORS

The following 15 items list some of the most frequent problems in temperament and self-regulation that parents and professionals observe in young children. Read each numbered item and check *No* if the behavior is not a problem. Check *Yes* if the behavior is a problem. Return this form to the individual administering this Screener for scoring and interpretation.

Name of rater: ______________________ Date Screener completed: ______________

Relationship to child: ______________________

	No	Yes
1. Emotions don't match what is going on	☐	☐
2. Gets angry too easily	☐	☐
3. Too easily frustrated	☐	☐
4. Has wild temper tantrums	☐	☐
5. Frequently irritable, "touchy," or fussy	☐	☐
6. Can't comfort self when upset	☐	☐
7. Doesn't pay attention to sights and sounds	☐	☐
8. Seems to look through or past people	☐	☐
9. Resists looking you in the eye	☐	☐
10. Too "grabby," impulsive	☐	☐
11. Moods and wants are too hard to figure out	☐	☐
12. Seems to be in "own world"	☐	☐
13. "Tunes out," loses contact with what is going on	☐	☐
14. Overexcited in crowded places	☐	☐
15. Wanders around without purpose	☐	☐

III. RESULTS

Add all the items marked *Yes*, and place the total in the box below labeled Raw Score. A score of 1or 2 indicates that the child may be at risk for atypical development and self-regulatory behavior. A score of 3 or more indicates that the child's temperament and self-regulatory behavior are probably atypical for his or her age. Follow-up with a complete 55-item TABS Assessment Tool is recommended for any score other than 0.

Raw Score ☐

Recommended for follow-up with TABS Assessment Tool: Yes ☐ No ☐

 ISBN-13: 978-1-55766-423-5 ISBN-10: 1-55766-423-4
Manufactured in the United States of America.

TABS Screener

Temperament and Atypical Behavior Scale

Early Childhood Indicators of Developmental Dysfunction

Stephen J. Bagnato, Ed.D., N.C.S.P.	John T. Neisworth, Ph.D.
John Salvia, D.Ed.	Frances M. Hunt, Ph.D.

Instructions for administering the TABS Screener:

Please refer to Chapter 3 of the **TABS Manual** for important information before administering the TABS Screener. Complete (or have rater complete) the information in Section I. Read and discuss directions for Section II with the rater, making sure that he or she understands how to respond to the items. Ask the rater to return the Screener for scoring and interpretation when he or she has completed Section II.

I. CHILD INFORMATION

Name of child: ______________________ Sex: Female ❑ Male ❑

Date of birth: ______________________ Age (in years and months): ______________

Child's address: ______________________

Name of parent or primary caregiver in household: ______________________

Relationship to child: Mother ❑ Father ❑ Other ______________

Telephone number: ______________________ Best time to contact: ______________

List any previously identified problems or diagnoses for this child.

1. ______________________
2. ______________________
3. ______________________

1-800-638-3775 www.brookespublishing.com

II. TABS INDICATORS

The following 15 items list some of the most frequent problems in temperament and self-regulation that parents and professionals observe in young children. Read each numbered item and check *No* if the behavior is not a problem. Check *Yes* if the behavior is a problem. Return this form to the individual administering this Screener for scoring and interpretation.

Name of rater: ______________________ Date Screener completed: ______________

Relationship to child: ______________________________________

	No	Yes
1. Emotions don't match what is going on	☐	☐
2. Gets angry too easily	☐	☐
3. Too easily frustrated	☐	☐
4. Has wild temper tantrums	☐	☐
5. Frequently irritable, "touchy," or fussy	☐	☐
6. Can't comfort self when upset	☐	☐
7. Doesn't pay attention to sights and sounds	☐	☐
8. Seems to look through or past people	☐	☐
9. Resists looking you in the eye	☐	☐
10. Too "grabby," impulsive	☐	☐
11. Moods and wants are too hard to figure out	☐	☐
12. Seems to be in "own world"	☐	☐
13. "Tunes out," loses contact with what is going on	☐	☐
14. Overexcited in crowded places	☐	☐
15. Wanders around without purpose	☐	☐

III. RESULTS

Add all the items marked *Yes*, and place the total in the box below labeled Raw Score. A score of 1or 2 indicates that the child may be at risk for atypical development and self-regulatory behavior. A score of 3 or more indicates that the child's temperament and self-regulatory behavior are probably atypical for his or her age. Follow-up with a complete 55-item TABS Assessment Tool is recommended for any score other than 0.

Raw Score ☐

Recommended for follow-up with TABS Assessment Tool: Yes ❑ No ❑

 ISBN-13: 978-1-55766-423-5 ISBN-10: 1-55766-423-4
Manufactured in the United States of America.

TABS Screener

Temperament and Atypical Behavior Scale

Early Childhood Indicators of Developmental Dysfunction

Stephen J. Bagnato, Ed.D., N.C.S.P.
John T. Neisworth, Ph.D.
John Salvia, D.Ed.
Frances M. Hunt, Ph.D.

Instructions for administering the TABS Screener:

Please refer to Chapter 3 of the **TABS Manual** for important information before administering the TABS Screener. Complete (or have rater complete) the information in Section I. Read and discuss directions for Section II with the rater, making sure that he or she understands how to respond to the items. Ask the rater to return the Screener for scoring and interpretation when he or she has completed Section II.

I. CHILD INFORMATION

Name of child: ______________________ Sex: Female ❑ Male ❑

Date of birth: ______________________ Age (in years and months): ______________

Child's address: ____

Name of parent or primary caregiver in household: ______________________

Relationship to child: Mother ❑ Father ❑ Other ______________________

Telephone number: ______________________ Best time to contact: ______________

List any previously identified problems or diagnoses for this child.

1. ____
2. ____
3. ____

1-800-638-3775 www.brookespublishing.com

II. TABS INDICATORS

The following 15 items list some of the most frequent problems in temperament and self-regulation that parents and professionals observe in young children. Read each numbered item and check *No* if the behavior is not a problem. Check *Yes* if the behavior is a problem. Return this form to the individual administering this Screener for scoring and interpretation.

Name of rater: ______________________ Date Screener completed: ____________

Relationship to child: ______________________________

	No	Yes
1. Emotions don't match what is going on	☐	☐
2. Gets angry too easily	☐	☐
3. Too easily frustrated	☐	☐
4. Has wild temper tantrums	☐	☐
5. Frequently irritable, "touchy," or fussy	☐	☐
6. Can't comfort self when upset	☐	☐
7. Doesn't pay attention to sights and sounds	☐	☐
8. Seems to look through or past people	☐	☐
9. Resists looking you in the eye	☐	☐
10. Too "grabby," impulsive	☐	☐
11. Moods and wants are too hard to figure out	☐	☐
12. Seems to be in "own world"	☐	☐
13. "Tunes out," loses contact with what is going on	☐	☐
14. Overexcited in crowded places	☐	☐
15. Wanders around without purpose	☐	☐

III. RESULTS

Add all the items marked *Yes*, and place the total in the box below labeled Raw Score. A score of 1or 2 indicates that the child may be at risk for atypical development and self-regulatory behavior. A score of 3 or more indicates that the child's temperament and self-regulatory behavior are probably atypical for his or her age. Follow-up with a complete 55-item TABS Assessment Tool is recommended for any score other than 0.

Raw Score ☐

Recommended for follow-up with TABS Assessment Tool: Yes ☐ No ☐

 ISBN-13: 978-1-55766-423-5 ISBN-10: 1-55766-423-4
Manufactured in the United States of America.

TABS Screener

Temperament and Atypical Behavior Scale

Early Childhood Indicators of Developmental Dysfunction

Stephen J. Bagnato, Ed.D., N.C.S.P. John T. Neisworth, Ph.D.

John Salvia, D.Ed. Frances M. Hunt, Ph.D.

Instructions for administering the TABS Screener:

Please refer to Chapter 3 of the **TABS Manual** for important information before administering the TABS Screener. Complete (or have rater complete) the information in Section I. Read and discuss directions for Section II with the rater, making sure that he or she understands how to respond to the items. Ask the rater to return the Screener for scoring and interpretation when he or she has completed Section II.

I. CHILD INFORMATION

Name of child: ______________________ Sex: Female ❑ Male ❑

Date of birth: ______________________ Age (in years and months): ______________________

Child's address: ______________________

Name of parent or primary caregiver in household: ______________________

Relationship to child: Mother ❑ Father ❑ Other ______________________

Telephone number: ______________________ Best time to contact: ______________________

List any previously identified problems or diagnoses for this child.

1. ______________________
2. ______________________
3. ______________________

1-800-638-3775 www.brookespublishing.com

II. TABS INDICATORS

The following 15 items list some of the most frequent problems in temperament and self-regulation that parents and professionals observe in young children. Read each numbered item and check *No* if the behavior is not a problem. Check *Yes* if the behavior is a problem. Return this form to the individual administering this Screener for scoring and interpretation.

Name of rater: ______________________ Date Screener completed: ______________

Relationship to child: ____

	No	Yes
1. Emotions don't match what is going on	☐	☐
2. Gets angry too easily	☐	☐
3. Too easily frustrated	☐	☐
4. Has wild temper tantrums	☐	☐
5. Frequently irritable, "touchy," or fussy	☐	☐
6. Can't comfort self when upset	☐	☐
7. Doesn't pay attention to sights and sounds	☐	☐
8. Seems to look through or past people	☐	☐
9. Resists looking you in the eye	☐	☐
10. Too "grabby," impulsive	☐	☐
11. Moods and wants are too hard to figure out	☐	☐
12. Seems to be in "own world"	☐	☐
13. "Tunes out," loses contact with what is going on	☐	☐
14. Overexcited in crowded places	☐	☐
15. Wanders around without purpose	☐	☐

III. RESULTS

Add all the items marked *Yes*, and place the total in the box below labeled Raw Score. A score of 1or 2 indicates that the child may be at risk for atypical development and self-regulatory behavior. A score of 3 or more indicates that the child's temperament and self-regulatory behavior are probably atypical for his or her age. Follow-up with a complete 55-item TABS Assessment Tool is recommended for any score other than 0.

Raw Score ☐

Recommended for follow-up with TABS Assessment Tool: Yes ☐ No ☐

 ISBN-13: 978-1-55766-423-5 ISBN-10: 1-55766-423-4
Manufactured in the United States of America.

TABS Screener

Temperament and Atypical Behavior Scale

Early Childhood Indicators of Developmental Dysfunction

Stephen J. Bagnato, Ed.D., N.C.S.P.
John T. Neisworth, Ph.D.
John Salvia, D.Ed.
Frances M. Hunt, Ph.D.

Instructions for administering the TABS Screener:

Please refer to Chapter 3 of the **TABS Manual** for important information before administering the TABS Screener. Complete (or have rater complete) the information in Section I. Read and discuss directions for Section II with the rater, making sure that he or she understands how to respond to the items. Ask the rater to return the Screener for scoring and interpretation when he or she has completed Section II.

I. CHILD INFORMATION

Name of child: ______________________ Sex: Female ❑ Male ❑

Date of birth: ______________________ Age (in years and months): ______________

Child's address: ______________________

Name of parent or primary caregiver in household: ______________________

Relationship to child: Mother ❑ Father ❑ Other ______________________

Telephone number: ______________________ Best time to contact: ______________

List any previously identified problems or diagnoses for this child.

1. ______________________
2. ______________________
3. ______________________

II. TABS INDICATORS

The following 15 items list some of the most frequent problems in temperament and self-regulation that parents and professionals observe in young children. Read each numbered item and check *No* if the behavior is not a problem. Check *Yes* if the behavior is a problem. Return this form to the individual administering this Screener for scoring and interpretation.

Name of rater: ______________________ Date Screener completed: ______________

Relationship to child: ______________________________________

	No	Yes
1. Emotions don't match what is going on	☐	☐
2. Gets angry too easily	☐	☐
3. Too easily frustrated	☐	☐
4. Has wild temper tantrums	☐	☐
5. Frequently irritable, "touchy," or fussy	☐	☐
6. Can't comfort self when upset	☐	☐
7. Doesn't pay attention to sights and sounds	☐	☐
8. Seems to look through or past people	☐	☐
9. Resists looking you in the eye	☐	☐
10. Too "grabby," impulsive	☐	☐
11. Moods and wants are too hard to figure out	☐	☐
12. Seems to be in "own world"	☐	☐
13. "Tunes out," loses contact with what is going on	☐	☐
14. Overexcited in crowded places	☐	☐
15. Wanders around without purpose	☐	☐

III. RESULTS

Add all the items marked *Yes*, and place the total in the box below labeled Raw Score. A score of 1or 2 indicates that the child may be at risk for atypical development and self-regulatory behavior. A score of 3 or more indicates that the child's temperament and self-regulatory behavior are probably atypical for his or her age. Follow-up with a complete 55-item TABS Assessment Tool is recommended for any score other than 0.

Raw Score ☐

Recommended for follow-up with TABS Assessment Tool: Yes ☐ No ☐

 ISBN-13: 978-1-55766-423-5 ISBN-10: 1-55766-423-4
Manufactured in the United States of America.

TABS Screener

Temperament and Atypical Behavior Scale

Early Childhood Indicators of Developmental Dysfunction

Stephen J. Bagnato, Ed.D., N.C.S.P. | John T. Neisworth, Ph.D.

John Salvia, D.Ed. | Frances M. Hunt, Ph.D.

Instructions for administering the TABS Screener:

Please refer to Chapter 3 of the **TABS Manual** for important information before administering the TABS Screener. Complete (or have rater complete) the information in Section I. Read and discuss directions for Section II with the rater, making sure that he or she understands how to respond to the items. Ask the rater to return the Screener for scoring and interpretation when he or she has completed Section II.

I. CHILD INFORMATION

Name of child: ______________________ Sex: Female ☐ Male ☐

Date of birth: ______________________ Age (in years and months): ______________

Child's address: ______________________

Name of parent or primary caregiver in household: ______________________

Relationship to child: Mother ☐ Father ☐ Other ______________________

Telephone number: ______________________ Best time to contact: ______________

List any previously identified problems or diagnoses for this child.

1. ______________________
2. ______________________
3. ______________________

1-800-638-3775 www.brookespublishing.com

II. TABS INDICATORS

The following 15 items list some of the most frequent problems in temperament and self-regulation that parents and professionals observe in young children. Read each numbered item and check *No* if the behavior is not a problem. Check *Yes* if the behavior is a problem. Return this form to the individual administering this Screener for scoring and interpretation.

Name of rater: ______________________ Date Screener completed: ____________

Relationship to child: ______________________________________

	No	Yes
1. Emotions don't match what is going on	☐	☐
2. Gets angry too easily	☐	☐
3. Too easily frustrated	☐	☐
4. Has wild temper tantrums	☐	☐
5. Frequently irritable, "touchy," or fussy	☐	☐
6. Can't comfort self when upset	☐	☐
7. Doesn't pay attention to sights and sounds	☐	☐
8. Seems to look through or past people	☐	☐
9. Resists looking you in the eye	☐	☐
10. Too "grabby," impulsive	☐	☐
11. Moods and wants are too hard to figure out	☐	☐
12. Seems to be in "own world"	☐	☐
13. "Tunes out," loses contact with what is going on	☐	☐
14. Overexcited in crowded places	☐	☐
15. Wanders around without purpose	☐	☐

III. RESULTS

Add all the items marked *Yes*, and place the total in the box below labeled Raw Score. A score of 1or 2 indicates that the child may be at risk for atypical development and self-regulatory behavior. A score of 3 or more indicates that the child's temperament and self-regulatory behavior are probably atypical for his or her age. Follow-up with a complete 55-item TABS Assessment Tool is recommended for any score other than 0.

Raw Score ☐

Recommended for follow-up with TABS Assessment Tool: Yes ☐ No ☐

 ISBN-13: 978-1-55766-423-5 ISBN-10: 1-55766-423-4
Manufactured in the United States of America.

TABS Screener

Temperament and Atypical Behavior Scale

Early Childhood Indicators of Developmental Dysfunction

Stephen J. Bagnato, Ed.D., N.C.S.P.
John T. Neisworth, Ph.D.
John Salvia, D.Ed.
Frances M. Hunt, Ph.D.

Instructions for administering the TABS Screener:

Please refer to Chapter 3 of the **TABS Manual** for important information before administering the TABS Screener. Complete (or have rater complete) the information in Section I. Read and discuss directions for Section II with the rater, making sure that he or she understands how to respond to the items. Ask the rater to return the Screener for scoring and interpretation when he or she has completed Section II.

I. CHILD INFORMATION

Name of child: ______________________ Sex: Female ❑ Male ❑

Date of birth: ______________________ Age (in years and months): ______________

Child's address: ______________________

Name of parent or primary caregiver in household: ______________________

Relationship to child: Mother ❑ Father ❑ Other ______________________

Telephone number: ______________________ Best time to contact: ______________

List any previously identified problems or diagnoses for this child.

1. ______________________
2. ______________________
3. ______________________

1-800-638-3775 www.brookespublishing.com

II. TABS INDICATORS

The following 15 items list some of the most frequent problems in temperament and self-regulation that parents and professionals observe in young children. Read each numbered item and check *No* if the behavior is not a problem. Check *Yes* if the behavior is a problem. Return this form to the individual administering this Screener for scoring and interpretation.

Name of rater: ______________________ Date Screener completed: ______________

Relationship to child: ______________________________________

	No	Yes
1. Emotions don't match what is going on	☐	☐
2. Gets angry too easily	☐	☐
3. Too easily frustrated	☐	☐
4. Has wild temper tantrums	☐	☐
5. Frequently irritable, "touchy," or fussy	☐	☐
6. Can't comfort self when upset	☐	☐
7. Doesn't pay attention to sights and sounds	☐	☐
8. Seems to look through or past people	☐	☐
9. Resists looking you in the eye	☐	☐
10. Too "grabby," impulsive	☐	☐
11. Moods and wants are too hard to figure out	☐	☐
12. Seems to be in "own world"	☐	☐
13. "Tunes out," loses contact with what is going on	☐	☐
14. Overexcited in crowded places	☐	☐
15. Wanders around without purpose	☐	☐

III. RESULTS

Add all the items marked *Yes*, and place the total in the box below labeled Raw Score. A score of 1or 2 indicates that the child may be at risk for atypical development and self-regulatory behavior. A score of 3 or more indicates that the child's temperament and self-regulatory behavior are probably atypical for his or her age. Follow-up with a complete 55-item TABS Assessment Tool is recommended for any score other than 0.

Raw Score ☐

Recommended for follow-up with TABS Assessment Tool: Yes ❑ No ❑

 ISBN-13: 978-1-55766-423-5 ISBN-10: 1-55766-423-4
Manufactured in the United States of America.

TABS Screener

Temperament and Atypical Behavior Scale

Early Childhood Indicators of Developmental Dysfunction

Stephen J. Bagnato, Ed.D., N.C.S.P.
John T. Neisworth, Ph.D.
John Salvia, D.Ed.
Frances M. Hunt, Ph.D.

Instructions for administering the TABS Screener:

Please refer to Chapter 3 of the **TABS Manual** for important information before administering the TABS Screener. Complete (or have rater complete) the information in Section I. Read and discuss directions for Section II with the rater, making sure that he or she understands how to respond to the items. Ask the rater to return the Screener for scoring and interpretation when he or she has completed Section II.

I. CHILD INFORMATION

Name of child: ______________________ Sex: Female ❑ Male ❑

Date of birth: ______________________ Age (in years and months): ______________

Child's address: ______________________

Name of parent or primary caregiver in household: ______________________

Relationship to child: Mother ❑ Father ❑ Other ______________________

Telephone number: ______________________ Best time to contact: ______________

List any previously identified problems or diagnoses for this child.

1. ______________________
2. ______________________
3. ______________________

II. TABS INDICATORS

The following 15 items list some of the most frequent problems in temperament and self-regulation that parents and professionals observe in young children. Read each numbered item and check *No* if the behavior is not a problem. Check *Yes* if the behavior is a problem. Return this form to the individual administering this Screener for scoring and interpretation.

Name of rater: ______________________ Date Screener completed: ______________

Relationship to child: ______________________________________

	No	Yes
1. Emotions don't match what is going on	☐	☐
2. Gets angry too easily	☐	☐
3. Too easily frustrated	☐	☐
4. Has wild temper tantrums	☐	☐
5. Frequently irritable, "touchy," or fussy	☐	☐
6. Can't comfort self when upset	☐	☐
7. Doesn't pay attention to sights and sounds	☐	☐
8. Seems to look through or past people	☐	☐
9. Resists looking you in the eye	☐	☐
10. Too "grabby," impulsive	☐	☐
11. Moods and wants are too hard to figure out	☐	☐
12. Seems to be in "own world"	☐	☐
13. "Tunes out," loses contact with what is going on	☐	☐
14. Overexcited in crowded places	☐	☐
15. Wanders around without purpose	☐	☐

III. RESULTS

Add all the items marked *Yes*, and place the total in the box below labeled Raw Score. A score of 1or 2 indicates that the child may be at risk for atypical development and self-regulatory behavior. A score of 3 or more indicates that the child's temperament and self-regulatory behavior are probably atypical for his or her age. Follow-up with a complete 55-item TABS Assessment Tool is recommended for any score other than 0.

Raw Score ☐

Recommended for follow-up with TABS Assessment Tool: Yes ☐ No ☐

 ISBN-13: 978-1-55766-423-5 ISBN-10: 1-55766-423-4
Manufactured in the United States of America.

TABS Screener

Temperament and Atypical Behavior Scale

Early Childhood Indicators of Developmental Dysfunction

Stephen J. Bagnato, Ed.D., N.C.S.P. | John T. Neisworth, Ph.D.
John Salvia, D.Ed. | Frances M. Hunt, Ph.D.

Instructions for administering the TABS Screener:

Please refer to Chapter 3 of the **TABS Manual** for important information before administering the TABS Screener. Complete (or have rater complete) the information in Section I. Read and discuss directions for Section II with the rater, making sure that he or she understands how to respond to the items. Ask the rater to return the Screener for scoring and interpretation when he or she has completed Section II.

I. CHILD INFORMATION

Name of child: ______________________ Sex: Female ❑ Male ❑

Date of birth: ______________________ Age (in years and months): ______________

Child's address: ____

Name of parent or primary caregiver in household: ______________________

Relationship to child: Mother ❑ Father ❑ Other ______________________

Telephone number: ______________________ Best time to contact: ______________

List any previously identified problems or diagnoses for this child.

1. ____
2. ____
3. ____

1-800-638-3775 www.brookespublishing.com

II. TABS INDICATORS

The following 15 items list some of the most frequent problems in temperament and self-regulation that parents and professionals observe in young children. Read each numbered item and check *No* if the behavior is not a problem. Check *Yes* if the behavior is a problem. Return this form to the individual administering this Screener for scoring and interpretation.

Name of rater: ______________________ Date Screener completed: ______________

Relationship to child: ______________________________________

	No	Yes
1. Emotions don't match what is going on	☐	☐
2. Gets angry too easily	☐	☐
3. Too easily frustrated	☐	☐
4. Has wild temper tantrums	☐	☐
5. Frequently irritable, "touchy," or fussy	☐	☐
6. Can't comfort self when upset	☐	☐
7. Doesn't pay attention to sights and sounds	☐	☐
8. Seems to look through or past people	☐	☐
9. Resists looking you in the eye	☐	☐
10. Too "grabby," impulsive	☐	☐
11. Moods and wants are too hard to figure out	☐	☐
12. Seems to be in "own world"	☐	☐
13. "Tunes out," loses contact with what is going on	☐	☐
14. Overexcited in crowded places	☐	☐
15. Wanders around without purpose	☐	☐

III. RESULTS

Add all the items marked *Yes*, and place the total in the box below labeled Raw Score. A score of 1or 2 indicates that the child may be at risk for atypical development and self-regulatory behavior. A score of 3 or more indicates that the child's temperament and self-regulatory behavior are probably atypical for his or her age. Follow-up with a complete 55-item TABS Assessment Tool is recommended for any score other than 0.

Raw Score ☐

Recommended for follow-up with TABS Assessment Tool: Yes ☐ No ☐

 ISBN-13: 978-1-55766-423-5 ISBN-10: 1-55766-423-4
Manufactured in the United States of America.

TABS Screener

Temperament and Atypical Behavior Scale

Early Childhood Indicators of Developmental Dysfunction

Stephen J. Bagnato, Ed.D., N.C.S.P. | John T. Neisworth, Ph.D.
John Salvia, D.Ed. | Frances M. Hunt, Ph.D.

Instructions for administering the TABS Screener:

Please refer to Chapter 3 of the **TABS Manual** for important information before administering the TABS Screener. Complete (or have rater complete) the information in Section I. Read and discuss directions for Section II with the rater, making sure that he or she understands how to respond to the items. Ask the rater to return the Screener for scoring and interpretation when he or she has completed Section II.

I. CHILD INFORMATION

Name of child: ______________________ Sex: Female ☐ Male ☐

Date of birth: ______________________ Age (in years and months): ______________

Child's address: ______________________

Name of parent or primary caregiver in household: ______________________

Relationship to child: Mother ☐ Father ☐ Other ______________________

Telephone number: ______________________ Best time to contact: ______________

List any previously identified problems or diagnoses for this child.

1. ______________________
2. ______________________
3. ______________________

1-800-638-3775 www.brookespublishing.com

II. TABS INDICATORS

The following 15 items list some of the most frequent problems in temperament and self-regulation that parents and professionals observe in young children. Read each numbered item and check *No* if the behavior is not a problem. Check *Yes* if the behavior is a problem. Return this form to the individual administering this Screener for scoring and interpretation.

Name of rater: ______________________ Date Screener completed: ______________

Relationship to child: ______________________________________

	No	Yes
1. Emotions don't match what is going on	☐	☐
2. Gets angry too easily	☐	☐
3. Too easily frustrated	☐	☐
4. Has wild temper tantrums	☐	☐
5. Frequently irritable, "touchy," or fussy	☐	☐
6. Can't comfort self when upset	☐	☐
7. Doesn't pay attention to sights and sounds	☐	☐
8. Seems to look through or past people	☐	☐
9. Resists looking you in the eye	☐	☐
10. Too "grabby," impulsive	☐	☐
11. Moods and wants are too hard to figure out	☐	☐
12. Seems to be in "own world"	☐	☐
13. "Tunes out," loses contact with what is going on	☐	☐
14. Overexcited in crowded places	☐	☐
15. Wanders around without purpose	☐	☐

III. RESULTS

Add all the items marked *Yes*, and place the total in the box below labeled Raw Score. A score of 1or 2 indicates that the child may be at risk for atypical development and self-regulatory behavior. A score of 3 or more indicates that the child's temperament and self-regulatory behavior are probably atypical for his or her age. Follow-up with a complete 55-item TABS Assessment Tool is recommended for any score other than 0.

Raw Score ☐

Recommended for follow-up with TABS Assessment Tool: Yes ❑ No ❑

 ISBN-13: 978-1-55766-423-5 ISBN-10: 1-55766-423-4
Manufactured in the United States of America.

TABS Screener

Temperament and Atypical Behavior Scale

Early Childhood Indicators of Developmental Dysfunction

Stephen J. Bagnato, Ed.D., N.C.S.P.	John T. Neisworth, Ph.D.
John Salvia, D.Ed.	Frances M. Hunt, Ph.D.

Instructions for administering the TABS Screener:

Please refer to Chapter 3 of the **TABS Manual** for important information before administering the TABS Screener. Complete (or have rater complete) the information in Section I. Read and discuss directions for Section II with the rater, making sure that he or she understands how to respond to the items. Ask the rater to return the Screener for scoring and interpretation when he or she has completed Section II.

I. CHILD INFORMATION

Name of child: ____________________ Sex: Female ❑ Male ❑

Date of birth: ____________________ Age (in years and months): ____________________

Child's address: ____________________

Name of parent or primary caregiver in household: ____________________

Relationship to child: Mother ❑ Father ❑ Other ____________________

Telephone number: ____________________ Best time to contact: ____________________

List any previously identified problems or diagnoses for this child.

1. ____________________
2. ____________________
3. ____________________

II. TABS INDICATORS

The following 15 items list some of the most frequent problems in temperament and self-regulation that parents and professionals observe in young children. Read each numbered item and check *No* if the behavior is not a problem. Check *Yes* if the behavior is a problem. Return this form to the individual administering this Screener for scoring and interpretation.

Name of rater: ______________________ Date Screener completed: ______________

Relationship to child: ______________________________________

	No	Yes
1. Emotions don't match what is going on	☐	☐
2. Gets angry too easily	☐	☐
3. Too easily frustrated	☐	☐
4. Has wild temper tantrums	☐	☐
5. Frequently irritable, "touchy," or fussy	☐	☐
6. Can't comfort self when upset	☐	☐
7. Doesn't pay attention to sights and sounds	☐	☐
8. Seems to look through or past people	☐	☐
9. Resists looking you in the eye	☐	☐
10. Too "grabby," impulsive	☐	☐
11. Moods and wants are too hard to figure out	☐	☐
12. Seems to be in "own world"	☐	☐
13. "Tunes out," loses contact with what is going on	☐	☐
14. Overexcited in crowded places	☐	☐
15. Wanders around without purpose	☐	☐

III. RESULTS

Add all the items marked *Yes*, and place the total in the box below labeled Raw Score. A score of 1or 2 indicates that the child may be at risk for atypical development and self-regulatory behavior. A score of 3 or more indicates that the child's temperament and self-regulatory behavior are probably atypical for his or her age. Follow-up with a complete 55-item TABS Assessment Tool is recommended for any score other than 0.

Raw Score ☐   Recommended for follow-up with TABS Assessment Tool: Yes ☐ No ☐

 ISBN-13: 978-1-55766-423-5 ISBN-10: 1-55766-423-4
Manufactured in the United States of America.

TABS Screener

Temperament and Atypical Behavior Scale

Early Childhood Indicators of Developmental Dysfunction

Stephen J. Bagnato, Ed.D., N.C.S.P.	John T. Neisworth, Ph.D.
John Salvia, D.Ed.	Frances M. Hunt, Ph.D.

Instructions for administering the TABS Screener:

Please refer to Chapter 3 of the **TABS Manual** for important information before administering the TABS Screener. Complete (or have rater complete) the information in Section I. Read and discuss directions for Section II with the rater, making sure that he or she understands how to respond to the items. Ask the rater to return the Screener for scoring and interpretation when he or she has completed Section II.

I. CHILD INFORMATION

Name of child: ______________________ Sex: Female ❑ Male ❑

Date of birth: ______________________ Age (in years and months): ______________

Child's address: ______________________

Name of parent or primary caregiver in household: ______________________

Relationship to child: Mother ❑ Father ❑ Other ______________________

Telephone number: ______________________ Best time to contact: ______________

List any previously identified problems or diagnoses for this child.

1. ______________________
2. ______________________
3. ______________________

II. TABS INDICATORS

The following 15 items list some of the most frequent problems in temperament and self-regulation that parents and professionals observe in young children. Read each numbered item and check *No* if the behavior is not a problem. Check *Yes* if the behavior is a problem. Return this form to the individual administering this Screener for scoring and interpretation.

Name of rater: ______________________ Date Screener completed: ______________

Relationship to child: ______________________________________

	No	Yes
1. Emotions don't match what is going on	☐	☐
2. Gets angry too easily	☐	☐
3. Too easily frustrated	☐	☐
4. Has wild temper tantrums	☐	☐
5. Frequently irritable, "touchy," or fussy	☐	☐
6. Can't comfort self when upset	☐	☐
7. Doesn't pay attention to sights and sounds	☐	☐
8. Seems to look through or past people	☐	☐
9. Resists looking you in the eye	☐	☐
10. Too "grabby," impulsive	☐	☐
11. Moods and wants are too hard to figure out	☐	☐
12. Seems to be in "own world"	☐	☐
13. "Tunes out," loses contact with what is going on	☐	☐
14. Overexcited in crowded places	☐	☐
15. Wanders around without purpose	☐	☐

III. RESULTS

Add all the items marked *Yes*, and place the total in the box below labeled Raw Score. A score of 1or 2 indicates that the child may be at risk for atypical development and self-regulatory behavior. A score of 3 or more indicates that the child's temperament and self-regulatory behavior are probably atypical for his or her age. Follow-up with a complete 55-item TABS Assessment Tool is recommended for any score other than 0.

Raw Score ☐

Recommended for follow-up with TABS Assessment Tool: Yes ☐ No ☐

 ISBN-13: 978-1-55766-423-5 ISBN-10: 1-55766-423-4
Manufactured in the United States of America.

TABS Screener

Temperament and Atypical Behavior Scale

Early Childhood Indicators of Developmental Dysfunction

Stephen J. Bagnato, Ed.D., N.C.S.P.
John T. Neisworth, Ph.D.
John Salvia, D.Ed.
Frances M. Hunt, Ph.D.

Instructions for administering the TABS Screener:

Please refer to Chapter 3 of the **TABS Manual** for important information before administering the TABS Screener. Complete (or have rater complete) the information in Section I. Read and discuss directions for Section II with the rater, making sure that he or she understands how to respond to the items. Ask the rater to return the Screener for scoring and interpretation when he or she has completed Section II

I. CHILD INFORMATION

Name of child: ______________________ Sex: Female ❑ Male ❑

Date of birth: ______________________ Age (in years and months): ______________________

Child's address: ______________________

Name of parent or primary caregiver in household: ______________________

Relationship to child: Mother ❑ Father ❑ Other ______________________

Telephone number: ______________________ Best time to contact: ______________________

List any previously identified problems or diagnoses for this child.

1. ______________________
2. ______________________
3. ______________________

1-800-638-3775 www.brookespublishing.com

II. TABS INDICATORS

The following 15 items list some of the most frequent problems in temperament and self-regulation that parents and professionals observe in young children. Read each numbered item and check *No* if the behavior is not a problem. Check *Yes* if the behavior is a problem. Return this form to the individual administering this Screener for scoring and interpretation.

Name of rater: ______________________ Date Screener completed: ______________

Relationship to child: ______________________________________

	No	Yes
1. Emotions don't match what is going on	☐	☐
2. Gets angry too easily	☐	☐
3. Too easily frustrated	☐	☐
4. Has wild temper tantrums	☐	☐
5. Frequently irritable, "touchy," or fussy	☐	☐
6. Can't comfort self when upset	☐	☐
7. Doesn't pay attention to sights and sounds	☐	☐
8. Seems to look through or past people	☐	☐
9. Resists looking you in the eye	☐	☐
10. Too "grabby," impulsive	☐	☐
11. Moods and wants are too hard to figure out	☐	☐
12. Seems to be in "own world"	☐	☐
13. "Tunes out," loses contact with what is going on	☐	☐
14. Overexcited in crowded places	☐	☐
15. Wanders around without purpose	☐	☐

III. RESULTS

Add all the items marked *Yes*, and place the total in the box below labeled Raw Score. A score of 1or 2 indicates that the child may be at risk for atypical development and self-regulatory behavior. A score of 3 or more indicates that the child's temperament and self-regulatory behavior are probably atypical for his or her age. Follow-up with a complete 55-item TABS Assessment Tool is recommended for any score other than 0.

Raw Score ☐

Recommended for follow-up with TABS Assessment Tool: Yes ❑ No ❑

 ISBN-13: 978-1-55766-423-5 ISBN-10: 1-55766-423-4
Manufactured in the United States of America.

TABS Screener

Temperament and Atypical Behavior Scale

Early Childhood Indicators of Developmental Dysfunction

Stephen J. Bagnato, Ed.D., N.C.S.P.	John T. Neisworth, Ph.D.
John Salvia, D.Ed.	Frances M. Hunt, Ph.D.

Instructions for administering the TABS Screener:

Please refer to Chapter 3 of the **TABS Manual** for important information before administering the TABS Screener. Complete (or have rater complete) the information in Section I. Read and discuss directions for Section II with the rater, making sure that he or she understands how to respond to the items. Ask the rater to return the Screener for scoring and interpretation when he or she has completed Section II.

I. CHILD INFORMATION

Name of child: ______________________ Sex: Female ❑ Male ❑

Date of birth: ______________________ Age (in years and months): ______________

Child's address: ______________________

Name of parent or primary caregiver in household: ______________________

Relationship to child: Mother ❑ Father ❑ Other ______________________

Telephone number: ______________________ Best time to contact: ______________

List any previously identified problems or diagnoses for this child.

1. ______________________
2. ______________________
3. ______________________

1-800-638-3775 www.brookespublishing.com

II. TABS INDICATORS

The following 15 items list some of the most frequent problems in temperament and self-regulation that parents and professionals observe in young children. Read each numbered item and check *No* if the behavior is not a problem. Check *Yes* if the behavior is a problem. Return this form to the individual administering this Screener for scoring and interpretation.

Name of rater: ________________________ Date Screener completed: ____________

Relationship to child: ____

	No	Yes
1. Emotions don't match what is going on	☐	☐
2. Gets angry too easily	☐	☐
3. Too easily frustrated	☐	☐
4. Has wild temper tantrums	☐	☐
5. Frequently irritable, "touchy," or fussy	☐	☐
6. Can't comfort self when upset	☐	☐
7. Doesn't pay attention to sights and sounds	☐	☐
8. Seems to look through or past people	☐	☐
9. Resists looking you in the eye	☐	☐
10. Too "grabby," impulsive	☐	☐
11. Moods and wants are too hard to figure out	☐	☐
12. Seems to be in "own world"	☐	☐
13. "Tunes out," loses contact with what is going on	☐	☐
14. Overexcited in crowded places	☐	☐
15. Wanders around without purpose	☐	☐

III. RESULTS

Add all the items marked *Yes*, and place the total in the box below labeled Raw Score. A score of 1or 2 indicates that the child may be at risk for atypical development and self-regulatory behavior. A score of 3 or more indicates that the child's temperament and self-regulatory behavior are probably atypical for his or her age. Follow-up with a complete 55-item TABS Assessment Tool is recommended for any score other than 0.

Raw Score ☐

Recommended for follow-up with TABS Assessment Tool: Yes ❑ No ❑

 ISBN-13: 978-1-55766-423-5 ISBN-10: 1-55766-423-4
Manufactured in the United States of America.

TABS Screener

Temperament and Atypical Behavior Scale

Early Childhood Indicators of Developmental Dysfunction

Stephen J. Bagnato, Ed.D., N.C.S.P.	John T. Neisworth, Ph.D.
John Salvia, D.Ed.	Frances M. Hunt, Ph.D.

Instructions for administering the TABS Screener:

Please refer to Chapter 3 of the **TABS Manual** for important information before administering the TABS Screener. Complete (or have rater complete) the information in Section I. Read and discuss directions for Section II with the rater, making sure that he or she understands how to respond to the items. Ask the rater to return the Screener for scoring and interpretation when he or she has completed Section II.

I. CHILD INFORMATION

Name of child: ______________________ Sex: Female ❑ Male ❑

Date of birth: ______________________ Age (in years and months): ______________________

Child's address: ______________________

Name of parent or primary caregiver in household: ______________________

Relationship to child: Mother ❑ Father ❑ Other ______________________

Telephone number: ______________________ Best time to contact: ______________________

List any previously identified problems or diagnoses for this child.

1. ______________________
2. ______________________
3. ______________________

1-800-638-3775 www.brookespublishing.com

II. TABS INDICATORS

The following 15 items list some of the most frequent problems in temperament and self-regulation that parents and professionals observe in young children. Read each numbered item and check *No* if the behavior is not a problem. Check *Yes* if the behavior is a problem. Return this form to the individual administering this Screener for scoring and interpretation.

Name of rater: ______________________ Date Screener completed: ______________

Relationship to child: ____

	No	Yes
1. Emotions don't match what is going on	☐	☐
2. Gets angry too easily	☐	☐
3. Too easily frustrated	☐	☐
4. Has wild temper tantrums	☐	☐
5. Frequently irritable, "touchy," or fussy	☐	☐
6. Can't comfort self when upset	☐	☐
7. Doesn't pay attention to sights and sounds	☐	☐
8. Seems to look through or past people	☐	☐
9. Resists looking you in the eye	☐	☐
10. Too "grabby," impulsive	☐	☐
11. Moods and wants are too hard to figure out	☐	☐
12. Seems to be in "own world"	☐	☐
13. "Tunes out," loses contact with what is going on	☐	☐
14. Overexcited in crowded places	☐	☐
15. Wanders around without purpose	☐	☐

III. RESULTS

Add all the items marked *Yes*, and place the total in the box below labeled Raw Score. A score of 1or 2 indicates that the child may be at risk for atypical development and self-regulatory behavior. A score of 3 or more indicates that the child's temperament and self-regulatory behavior are probably atypical for his or her age. Follow-up with a complete 55-item TABS Assessment Tool is recommended for any score other than 0.

Raw Score ☐

Recommended for follow-up with TABS Assessment Tool: Yes ☐ No ☐

ISBN-13: 978-1-55766-423-5 ISBN-10: 1-55766-423-4
Manufactured in the United States of America.

TABS Screener

Temperament and Atypical Behavior Scale

Early Childhood Indicators of Developmental Dysfunction

Stephen J. Bagnato, Ed.D., N.C.S.P.
John T. Neisworth, Ph.D.
John Salvia, D.Ed.
Frances M. Hunt, Ph.D.

Instructions for administering the TABS Screener:

Please refer to Chapter 3 of the **TABS Manual** for important information before administering the TABS Screener. Complete (or have rater complete) the information in Section I. Read and discuss directions for Section II with the rater, making sure that he or she understands how to respond to the items. Ask the rater to return the Screener for scoring and interpretation when he or she has completed Section II.

I. CHILD INFORMATION

Name of child: ______________________ Sex: Female ☐ Male ☐

Date of birth: ______________________ Age (in years and months): ______________

Child's address: ____

Name of parent or primary caregiver in household: ______________________

Relationship to child: Mother ☐ Father ☐ Other ______________________

Telephone number: ______________________ Best time to contact: ______________

List any previously identified problems or diagnoses for this child.

1. ____
2. ____
3. ____

1-800-638-3775 www.brookespublishing.com

II. TABS INDICATORS

The following 15 items list some of the most frequent problems in temperament and self-regulation that parents and professionals observe in young children. Read each numbered item and check *No* if the behavior is not a problem. Check *Yes* if the behavior is a problem. Return this form to the individual administering this Screener for scoring and interpretation.

Name of rater: ______________________ Date Screener completed: ____________

Relationship to child: ______________________________

	No	Yes
1. Emotions don't match what is going on	☐	☐
2. Gets angry too easily	☐	☐
3. Too easily frustrated	☐	☐
4. Has wild temper tantrums	☐	☐
5. Frequently irritable, "touchy," or fussy	☐	☐
6. Can't comfort self when upset	☐	☐
7. Doesn't pay attention to sights and sounds	☐	☐
8. Seems to look through or past people	☐	☐
9. Resists looking you in the eye	☐	☐
10. Too "grabby," impulsive	☐	☐
11. Moods and wants are too hard to figure out	☐	☐
12. Seems to be in "own world"	☐	☐
13. "Tunes out," loses contact with what is going on	☐	☐
14. Overexcited in crowded places	☐	☐
15. Wanders around without purpose	☐	☐

III. RESULTS

Add all the items marked *Yes*, and place the total in the box below labeled Raw Score. A score of 1or 2 indicates that the child may be at risk for atypical development and self-regulatory behavior. A score of 3 or more indicates that the child's temperament and self-regulatory behavior are probably atypical for his or her age. Follow-up with a complete 55-item TABS Assessment Tool is recommended for any score other than 0.

Raw Score ☐

Recommended for follow-up with TABS Assessment Tool: Yes ☐ No ☐

 ISBN-13: 978-1-55766-423-5 ISBN-10: 1-55766-423-4
Manufactured in the United States of America.

TABS Screener

Temperament and Atypical Behavior Scale

Early Childhood Indicators of Developmental Dysfunction

Stephen J. Bagnato, Ed.D., N.C.S.P. | John T. Neisworth, Ph.D.
John Salvia, D.Ed. | Frances M. Hunt, Ph.D.

Instructions for administering the TABS Screener:

Please refer to Chapter 3 of the **TABS Manual** for important information before administering the TABS Screener. Complete (or have rater complete) the information in Section I. Read and discuss directions for Section II with the rater, making sure that he or she understands how to respond to the items. Ask the rater to return the Screener for scoring and interpretation when he or she has completed Section II.

I. CHILD INFORMATION

Name of child: ______________________ Sex: Female ❑ Male ❑

Date of birth: ______________________ Age (in years and months): ______________

Child's address: ______________________

Name of parent or primary caregiver in household: ______________________

Relationship to child: Mother ❑ Father ❑ Other ______________________

Telephone number: ______________________ Best time to contact: ______________

List any previously identified problems or diagnoses for this child.

1. ______________________
2. ______________________
3. ______________________

1-800-638-3775 www.brookespublishing.com

II. TABS INDICATORS

The following 15 items list some of the most frequent problems in temperament and self-regulation that parents and professionals observe in young children. Read each numbered item and check *No* if the behavior is not a problem. Check *Yes* if the behavior is a problem. Return this form to the individual administering this Screener for scoring and interpretation.

Name of rater: ______________________________ Date Screener completed: ______________

Relationship to child: ____

	No	Yes
1. Emotions don't match what is going on	☐	☐
2. Gets angry too easily	☐	☐
3. Too easily frustrated	☐	☐
4. Has wild temper tantrums	☐	☐
5. Frequently irritable, "touchy," or fussy	☐	☐
6. Can't comfort self when upset	☐	☐
7. Doesn't pay attention to sights and sounds	☐	☐
8. Seems to look through or past people	☐	☐
9. Resists looking you in the eye	☐	☐
10. Too "grabby," impulsive	☐	☐
11. Moods and wants are too hard to figure out	☐	☐
12. Seems to be in "own world"	☐	☐
13. "Tunes out," loses contact with what is going on	☐	☐
14. Overexcited in crowded places	☐	☐
15. Wanders around without purpose	☐	☐

III. RESULTS

Add all the items marked *Yes*, and place the total in the box below labeled Raw Score. A score of 1or 2 indicates that the child may be at risk for atypical development and self-regulatory behavior. A score of 3 or more indicates that the child's temperament and self-regulatory behavior are probably atypical for his or her age. Follow-up with a complete 55-item TABS Assessment Tool is recommended for any score other than 0.

Raw Score ☐

Recommended for follow-up with TABS Assessment Tool: Yes ☐ No ☐

 ISBN-13: 978-1-55766-423-5 ISBN-10: 1-55766-423-4
Manufactured in the United States of America.

TABS Screener

Temperament and Atypical Behavior Scale

Early Childhood Indicators of Developmental Dysfunction

Stephen J. Bagnato, Ed.D., N.C.S.P. | John T. Neisworth, Ph.D.
John Salvia, D.Ed. | Frances M. Hunt, Ph.D.

Instructions for administering the TABS Screener:

Please refer to Chapter 3 of the **TABS Manual** for important information before administering the TABS Screener. Complete (or have rater complete) the information in Section I. Read and discuss directions for Section II with the rater, making sure that he or she understands how to respond to the items. Ask the rater to return the Screener for scoring and interpretation when he or she has completed Section II.

I. CHILD INFORMATION

Name of child: ______________________ Sex: Female ❑ Male ❑

Date of birth: ______________________ Age (in years and months): ______________

Child's address: ______________________

Name of parent or primary caregiver in household: ______________________

Relationship to child: Mother ❑ Father ❑ Other ______________________

Telephone number: ______________________ Best time to contact: ______________

List any previously identified problems or diagnoses for this child.

1. ______________________
2. ______________________
3. ______________________

1-800-638-3775 www.brookespublishing.com

II. TABS INDICATORS

The following 15 items list some of the most frequent problems in temperament and self-regulation that parents and professionals observe in young children. Read each numbered item and check *No* if the behavior is not a problem. Check *Yes* if the behavior is a problem. Return this form to the individual administering this Screener for scoring and interpretation.

Name of rater: ______________________ Date Screener completed: ______________

Relationship to child: ______________________________________

	No	Yes
1. Emotions don't match what is going on	☐	☐
2. Gets angry too easily	☐	☐
3. Too easily frustrated	☐	☐
4. Has wild temper tantrums	☐	☐
5. Frequently irritable, "touchy," or fussy	☐	☐
6. Can't comfort self when upset	☐	☐
7. Doesn't pay attention to sights and sounds	☐	☐
8. Seems to look through or past people	☐	☐
9. Resists looking you in the eye	☐	☐
10. Too "grabby," impulsive	☐	☐
11. Moods and wants are too hard to figure out	☐	☐
12. Seems to be in "own world"	☐	☐
13. "Tunes out," loses contact with what is going on	☐	☐
14. Overexcited in crowded places	☐	☐
15. Wanders around without purpose	☐	☐

III. RESULTS

Add all the items marked *Yes*, and place the total in the box below labeled Raw Score. A score of 1or 2 indicates that the child may be at risk for atypical development and self-regulatory behavior. A score of 3 or more indicates that the child's temperament and self-regulatory behavior are probably atypical for his or her age. Follow-up with a complete 55-item TABS Assessment Tool is recommended for any score other than 0.

Raw Score ☐

Recommended for follow-up with TABS Assessment Tool: Yes ☐ No ☐

 ISBN-13: 978-1-55766-423-5 ISBN-10: 1-55766-423-4
Manufactured in the United States of America.

TABS Screener

Temperament and Atypical Behavior Scale

Early Childhood Indicators of Developmental Dysfunction

Stephen J. Bagnato, Ed.D., N.C.S.P.
John T. Neisworth, Ph.D.
John Salvia, D.Ed.
Frances M. Hunt, Ph.D.

Instructions for administering the TABS Screener:

Please refer to Chapter 3 of the **TABS Manual** for important information before administering the TABS Screener. Complete (or have rater complete) the information in Section I. Read and discuss directions for Section II with the rater, making sure that he or she understands how to respond to the items. Ask the rater to return the Screener for scoring and interpretation when he or she has completed Section II.

I. CHILD INFORMATION

Name of child: ______________________ Sex: Female ❑ Male ❑

Date of birth: ______________________ Age (in years and months): ______________

Child's address: ______________________

Name of parent or primary caregiver in household: ______________________

Relationship to child: Mother ❑ Father ❑ Other ______________________

Telephone number: ______________________ Best time to contact: ______________

List any previously identified problems or diagnoses for this child.

1. ______________________
2. ______________________
3. ______________________

1-800-638-3775 www.brookespublishing.com

II. TABS INDICATORS

The following 15 items list some of the most frequent problems in temperament and self-regulation that parents and professionals observe in young children. Read each numbered item and check *No* if the behavior is not a problem. Check *Yes* if the behavior is a problem. Return this form to the individual administering this Screener for scoring and interpretation.

Name of rater: ____________________ Date Screener completed: ____________

Relationship to child: ____________________

	No	Yes
1. Emotions don't match what is going on	☐	☐
2. Gets angry too easily	☐	☐
3. Too easily frustrated	☐	☐
4. Has wild temper tantrums	☐	☐
5. Frequently irritable, "touchy," or fussy	☐	☐
6. Can't comfort self when upset	☐	☐
7. Doesn't pay attention to sights and sounds	☐	☐
8. Seems to look through or past people	☐	☐
9. Resists looking you in the eye	☐	☐
10. Too "grabby," impulsive	☐	☐
11. Moods and wants are too hard to figure out	☐	☐
12. Seems to be in "own world"	☐	☐
13. "Tunes out," loses contact with what is going on	☐	☐
14. Overexcited in crowded places	☐	☐
15. Wanders around without purpose	☐	☐

III. RESULTS

Add all the items marked *Yes*, and place the total in the box below labeled Raw Score. A score of 1or 2 indicates that the child may be at risk for atypical development and self-regulatory behavior. A score of 3 or more indicates that the child's temperament and self-regulatory behavior are probably atypical for his or her age. Follow-up with a complete 55-item TABS Assessment Tool is recommended for any score other than 0.

Raw Score ☐

Recommended for follow-up with TABS Assessment Tool: Yes ☐ No ☐

 ISBN-13: 978-1-55766-423-5 ISBN-10: 1-55766-423-4
Manufactured in the United States of America.

TABS Screener

Temperament and Atypical Behavior Scale

Early Childhood Indicators of Developmental Dysfunction

Stephen J. Bagnato, Ed.D., N.C.S.P.

John T. Neisworth, Ph.D.

John Salvia, D.Ed.

Frances M. Hunt, Ph.D.

Instructions for administering the TABS Screener:

Please refer to Chapter 3 of the **TABS Manual** for important information before administering the TABS Screener. Complete (or have rater complete) the information in Section I. Read and discuss directions for Section II with the rater, making sure that he or she understands how to respond to the items. Ask the rater to return the Screener for scoring and interpretation when he or she has completed Section II.

I. CHILD INFORMATION

Name of child: ______________________ Sex: Female ❑ Male ❑

Date of birth: ______________________ Age (in years and months): ______________________

Child's address: ______________________

Name of parent or primary caregiver in household: ______________________

Relationship to child: Mother ❑ Father ❑ Other ______________________

Telephone number: ______________________ Best time to contact: ______________________

List any previously identified problems or diagnoses for this child.

1. ______________________
2. ______________________
3. ______________________

1-800-638-3775 www.brookespublishing.com

II. TABS INDICATORS

The following 15 items list some of the most frequent problems in temperament and self-regulation that parents and professionals observe in young children. Read each numbered item and check *No* if the behavior is not a problem. Check *Yes* if the behavior is a problem. Return this form to the individual administering this Screener for scoring and interpretation.

Name of rater: ______________________ Date Screener completed: ______________

Relationship to child: ______________________________

	No	Yes
1. Emotions don't match what is going on	☐	☐
2. Gets angry too easily	☐	☐
3. Too easily frustrated	☐	☐
4. Has wild temper tantrums	☐	☐
5. Frequently irritable, "touchy," or fussy	☐	☐
6. Can't comfort self when upset	☐	☐
7. Doesn't pay attention to sights and sounds	☐	☐
8. Seems to look through or past people	☐	☐
9. Resists looking you in the eye	☐	☐
10. Too "grabby," impulsive	☐	☐
11. Moods and wants are too hard to figure out	☐	☐
12. Seems to be in "own world"	☐	☐
13. "Tunes out," loses contact with what is going on	☐	☐
14. Overexcited in crowded places	☐	☐
15. Wanders around without purpose	☐	☐

III. RESULTS

Add all the items marked *Yes*, and place the total in the box below labeled Raw Score. A score of 1or 2 indicates that the child may be at risk for atypical development and self-regulatory behavior. A score of 3 or more indicates that the child's temperament and self-regulatory behavior are probably atypical for his or her age. Follow-up with a complete 55-item TABS Assessment Tool is recommended for any score other than 0.

Raw Score ☐

Recommended for follow-up with TABS Assessment Tool: Yes ❑ No ❑

 ISBN-13: 978-1-55766-423-5 ISBN-10: 1-55766-423-4
Manufactured in the United States of America.

TABS Screener

Temperament and Atypical Behavior Scale

Early Childhood Indicators of Developmental Dysfunction

Stephen J. Bagnato, Ed.D., N.C.S.P. | John T. Neisworth, Ph.D.
John Salvia, D.Ed. | Frances M. Hunt, Ph.D.

Instructions for administering the TABS Screener:

Please refer to Chapter 3 of the **TABS Manual** for important information before administering the TABS Screener. Complete (or have rater complete) the information in Section I. Read and discuss directions for Section II with the rater, making sure that he or she understands how to respond to the items. Ask the rater to return the Screener for scoring and interpretation when he or she has completed Section II.

I. CHILD INFORMATION

Name of child: ______________________ Sex: Female ❑ Male ❑

Date of birth: ______________________ Age (in years and months): ______________

Child's address: ____

Name of parent or primary caregiver in household: ______________________

Relationship to child: Mother ❑ Father ❑ Other ______________________

Telephone number: ______________________ Best time to contact: ______________

List any previously identified problems or diagnoses for this child.

1. ____
2. ____
3. ____

1-800-638-3775 www.brookespublishing.com

II. TABS INDICATORS

The following 15 items list some of the most frequent problems in temperament and self-regulation that parents and professionals observe in young children. Read each numbered item and check *No* if the behavior is not a problem. Check *Yes* if the behavior is a problem. Return this form to the individual administering this Screener for scoring and interpretation.

Name of rater: ______________________ Date Screener completed: ______________

Relationship to child: ____

	No	Yes
1. Emotions don't match what is going on	☐	☐
2. Gets angry too easily	☐	☐
3. Too easily frustrated	☐	☐
4. Has wild temper tantrums	☐	☐
5. Frequently irritable, "touchy," or fussy	☐	☐
6. Can't comfort self when upset	☐	☐
7. Doesn't pay attention to sights and sounds	☐	☐
8. Seems to look through or past people	☐	☐
9. Resists looking you in the eye	☐	☐
10. Too "grabby," impulsive	☐	☐
11. Moods and wants are too hard to figure out	☐	☐
12. Seems to be in "own world"	☐	☐
13. "Tunes out," loses contact with what is going on	☐	☐
14. Overexcited in crowded places	☐	☐
15. Wanders around without purpose	☐	☐

III. RESULTS

Add all the items marked *Yes*, and place the total in the box below labeled Raw Score. A score of 1or 2 indicates that the child may be at risk for atypical development and self-regulatory behavior. A score of 3 or more indicates that the child's temperament and self-regulatory behavior are probably atypical for his or her age. Follow-up with a complete 55-item TABS Assessment Tool is recommended for any score other than 0.

Raw Score ☐

Recommended for follow-up with TABS Assessment Tool: Yes ❑ No ❑

 ISBN-13: 978-1-55766-423-5 ISBN-10: 1-55766-423-4
Manufactured in the United States of America.

TABS Screener

Temperament and Atypical Behavior Scale

Early Childhood Indicators of Developmental Dysfunction

Stephen J. Bagnato, Ed.D., N.C.S.P.
John T. Neisworth, Ph.D.
John Salvia, D.Ed.
Frances M. Hunt, Ph.D.

Instructions for administering the TABS Screener:

Please refer to Chapter 3 of the **TABS Manual** for important information before administering the TABS Screener. Complete (or have rater complete) the information in Section I. Read and discuss directions for Section II with the rater, making sure that he or she understands how to respond to the items. Ask the rater to return the Screener for scoring and interpretation when he or she has completed Section II.

I. CHILD INFORMATION

Name of child: ______________________ Sex: Female ☐ Male ☐

Date of birth: ______________________ Age (in years and months): ______________________

Child's address: ______________________

Name of parent or primary caregiver in household: ______________________

Relationship to child: Mother ☐ Father ☐ Other ______________________

Telephone number: ______________________ Best time to contact: ______________________

List any previously identified problems or diagnoses for this child.

1. ______________________
2. ______________________
3. ______________________

1-800-638-3775 www.brookespublishing.com

II. TABS INDICATORS

The following 15 items list some of the most frequent problems in temperament and self-regulation that parents and professionals observe in young children. Read each numbered item and check *No* if the behavior is not a problem. Check *Yes* if the behavior is a problem. Return this form to the individual administering this Screener for scoring and interpretation.

Name of rater: ______________________ Date Screener completed: ______________

Relationship to child: ______________________________________

	No	Yes
1. Emotions don't match what is going on	☐	☐
2. Gets angry too easily	☐	☐
3. Too easily frustrated	☐	☐
4. Has wild temper tantrums	☐	☐
5. Frequently irritable, "touchy," or fussy	☐	☐
6. Can't comfort self when upset	☐	☐
7. Doesn't pay attention to sights and sounds	☐	☐
8. Seems to look through or past people	☐	☐
9. Resists looking you in the eye	☐	☐
10. Too "grabby," impulsive	☐	☐
11. Moods and wants are too hard to figure out	☐	☐
12. Seems to be in "own world"	☐	☐
13. "Tunes out," loses contact with what is going on	☐	☐
14. Overexcited in crowded places	☐	☐
15. Wanders around without purpose	☐	☐

III. RESULTS

Add all the items marked *Yes*, and place the total in the box below labeled Raw Score. A score of 1or 2 indicates that the child may be at risk for atypical development and self-regulatory behavior. A score of 3 or more indicates that the child's temperament and self-regulatory behavior are probably atypical for his or her age. Follow-up with a complete 55-item TABS Assessment Tool is recommended for any score other than 0.

Raw Score ☐

Recommended for follow-up with TABS Assessment Tool: Yes ☐ No ☐

 ISBN-13: 978-1-55766-423-5 ISBN-10: 1-55766-423-4
Manufactured in the United States of America.

TABS Screener

Temperament and Atypical Behavior Scale

Early Childhood Indicators of Developmental Dysfunction

Stephen J. Bagnato, Ed.D., N.C.S.P. | John T. Neisworth, Ph.D.
John Salvia, D.Ed. | Frances M. Hunt, Ph.D.

Instructions for administering the TABS Screener:

Please refer to Chapter 3 of the **TABS Manual** for important information before administering the TABS Screener. Complete (or have rater complete) the information in Section I. Read and discuss directions for Section II with the rater, making sure that he or she understands how to respond to the items. Ask the rater to return the Screener for scoring and interpretation when he or she has completed Section II.

I. CHILD INFORMATION

Name of child: ____________________ Sex: Female ☐ Male ☐

Date of birth: ____________________ Age (in years and months): ____________________

Child's address: ____________________

Name of parent or primary caregiver in household: ____________________

Relationship to child: Mother ☐ Father ☐ Other ____________________

Telephone number: ____________________ Best time to contact: ____________________

List any previously identified problems or diagnoses for this child.

1. ____________________
2. ____________________
3. ____________________

1-800-638-3775 www.brookespublishing.com

II. TABS INDICATORS

The following 15 items list some of the most frequent problems in temperament and self-regulation that parents and professionals observe in young children. Read each numbered item and check *No* if the behavior is not a problem. Check *Yes* if the behavior is a problem. Return this form to the individual administering this Screener for scoring and interpretation.

Name of rater: ______________________________ Date Screener completed: ______________

Relationship to child: ____

	No	Yes
1. Emotions don't match what is going on	☐	☐
2. Gets angry too easily	☐	☐
3. Too easily frustrated	☐	☐
4. Has wild temper tantrums	☐	☐
5. Frequently irritable, "touchy," or fussy	☐	☐
6. Can't comfort self when upset	☐	☐
7. Doesn't pay attention to sights and sounds	☐	☐
8. Seems to look through or past people	☐	☐
9. Resists looking you in the eye	☐	☐
10. Too "grabby," impulsive	☐	☐
11. Moods and wants are too hard to figure out	☐	☐
12. Seems to be in "own world"	☐	☐
13. "Tunes out," loses contact with what is going on	☐	☐
14. Overexcited in crowded places	☐	☐
15. Wanders around without purpose	☐	☐

III. RESULTS

Add all the items marked *Yes*, and place the total in the box below labeled Raw Score. A score of 1or 2 indicates that the child may be at risk for atypical development and self-regulatory behavior. A score of 3 or more indicates that the child's temperament and self-regulatory behavior are probably atypical for his or her age. Follow-up with a complete 55-item TABS Assessment Tool is recommended for any score other than 0.

Raw Score ☐

Recommended for follow-up with TABS Assessment Tool: Yes ☐ No ☐

 ISBN-13: 978-1-55766-423-5 ISBN-10: 1-55766-423-4
Manufactured in the United States of America.

TABS Screener

Temperament and Atypical Behavior Scale

Early Childhood Indicators of Developmental Dysfunction

Stephen J. Bagnato, Ed.D., N.C.S.P. | John T. Neisworth, Ph.D.

John Salvia, D.Ed. | Frances M. Hunt, Ph.D.

Instructions for administering the TABS Screener:

Please refer to Chapter 3 of the **TABS Manual** for important information before administering the TABS Screener. Complete (or have rater complete) the information in Section I. Read and discuss directions for Section II with the rater, making sure that he or she understands how to respond to the items. Ask the rater to return the Screener for scoring and interpretation when he or she has completed Section II.

I. CHILD INFORMATION

Name of child: ______________________ Sex: Female ❑ Male ❑

Date of birth: ______________________ Age (in years and months): ______________________

Child's address: ______________________

Name of parent or primary caregiver in household: ______________________

Relationship to child: Mother ❑ Father ❑ Other ______________________

Telephone number: ______________________ Best time to contact: ______________________

List any previously identified problems or diagnoses for this child.

1. ______________________
2. ______________________
3. ______________________

1-800-638-3775 www.brookespublishing.com

II. TABS INDICATORS

The following 15 items list some of the most frequent problems in temperament and self-regulation that parents and professionals observe in young children. Read each numbered item and check *No* if the behavior is not a problem. Check *Yes* if the behavior is a problem. Return this form to the individual administering this Screener for scoring and interpretation.

Name of rater: ______________________ Date Screener completed: ______________

Relationship to child: ______________________________

	No	Yes
1. Emotions don't match what is going on	☐	☐
2. Gets angry too easily	☐	☐
3. Too easily frustrated	☐	☐
4. Has wild temper tantrums	☐	☐
5. Frequently irritable, "touchy," or fussy	☐	☐
6. Can't comfort self when upset	☐	☐
7. Doesn't pay attention to sights and sounds	☐	☐
8. Seems to look through or past people	☐	☐
9. Resists looking you in the eye	☐	☐
10. Too "grabby," impulsive	☐	☐
11. Moods and wants are too hard to figure out	☐	☐
12. Seems to be in "own world"	☐	☐
13. "Tunes out," loses contact with what is going on	☐	☐
14. Overexcited in crowded places	☐	☐
15. Wanders around without purpose	☐	☐

III. RESULTS

Add all the items marked *Yes*, and place the total in the box below labeled Raw Score. A score of 1or 2 indicates that the child may be at risk for atypical development and self-regulatory behavior. A score of 3 or more indicates that the child's temperament and self-regulatory behavior are probably atypical for his or her age. Follow-up with a complete 55-item TABS Assessment Tool is recommended for any score other than 0.

Raw Score ☐

Recommended for follow-up with TABS Assessment Tool: Yes ☐ No ☐

 ISBN-13: 978-1-55766-423-5 ISBN-10: 1-55766-423-4
Manufactured in the United States of America.

TABS Screener

Temperament and Atypical Behavior Scale

Early Childhood Indicators of Developmental Dysfunction

Stephen J. Bagnato, Ed.D., N.C.S.P.
John T. Neisworth, Ph.D.
John Salvia, D.Ed.
Frances M. Hunt, Ph.D.

Instructions for administering the TABS Screener:

Please refer to Chapter 3 of the **TABS Manual** for important information before administering the TABS Screener. Complete (or have rater complete) the information in Section I. Read and discuss directions for Section II with the rater, making sure that he or she understands how to respond to the items. Ask the rater to return the Screener for scoring and interpretation when he or she has completed Section II.

I. CHILD INFORMATION

Name of child: ______________________ Sex: Female ❑ Male ❑

Date of birth: ______________________ Age (in years and months): ______________________

Child's address: ______________________

Name of parent or primary caregiver in household: ______________________

Relationship to child: Mother ❑ Father ❑ Other ______________________

Telephone number: ______________________ Best time to contact: ______________________

List any previously identified problems or diagnoses for this child.

1. ______________________
2. ______________________
3. ______________________

1-800-638-3775 www.brookespublishing.com

II. TABS INDICATORS

The following 15 items list some of the most frequent problems in temperament and self-regulation that parents and professionals observe in young children. Read each numbered item and check *No* if the behavior is not a problem. Check *Yes* if the behavior is a problem. Return this form to the individual administering this Screener for scoring and interpretation.

Name of rater: ______________________________ Date Screener completed: ______________

Relationship to child: ____

	No	Yes
1. Emotions don't match what is going on	☐	☐
2. Gets angry too easily	☐	☐
3. Too easily frustrated	☐	☐
4. Has wild temper tantrums	☐	☐
5. Frequently irritable, "touchy," or fussy	☐	☐
6. Can't comfort self when upset	☐	☐
7. Doesn't pay attention to sights and sounds	☐	☐
8. Seems to look through or past people	☐	☐
9. Resists looking you in the eye	☐	☐
10. Too "grabby," impulsive	☐	☐
11. Moods and wants are too hard to figure out	☐	☐
12. Seems to be in "own world"	☐	☐
13. "Tunes out," loses contact with what is going on	☐	☐
14. Overexcited in crowded places	☐	☐
15. Wanders around without purpose	☐	☐

III. RESULTS

Add all the items marked *Yes*, and place the total in the box below labeled Raw Score. A score of 1or 2 indicates that the child may be at risk for atypical development and self-regulatory behavior. A score of 3 or more indicates that the child's temperament and self-regulatory behavior are probably atypical for his or her age. Follow-up with a complete 55-item TABS Assessment Tool is recommended for any score other than 0.

Raw Score ☐

Recommended for follow-up with TABS Assessment Tool: Yes ❑ No ❑

 ISBN-13: 978-1-55766-423-5 ISBN-10: 1-55766-423-4
Manufactured in the United States of America.

TABS Screener

Temperament and Atypical Behavior Scale

Early Childhood Indicators of Developmental Dysfunction

Stephen J. Bagnato, Ed.D., N.C.S.P. | John T. Neisworth, Ph.D.

John Salvia, D.Ed. | Frances M. Hunt, Ph.D.

Instructions for administering the TABS Screener:

Please refer to Chapter 3 of the **TABS Manual** for important information before administering the TABS Screener. Complete (or have rater complete) the information in Section I. Read and discuss directions for Section II with the rater, making sure that he or she understands how to respond to the items. Ask the rater to return the Screener for scoring and interpretation when he or she has completed Section II.

I. CHILD INFORMATION

Name of child: ______________________ Sex: Female ❑ Male ❑

Date of birth: ______________ Age (in years and months): ______________

Child's address: ______________________

Name of parent or primary caregiver in household: ______________________

Relationship to child: Mother ❑ Father ❑ Other ______________

Telephone number: ______________ Best time to contact: ______________

List any previously identified problems or diagnoses for this child.

1. ______________________
2. ______________________
3. ______________________

II. TABS INDICATORS

The following 15 items list some of the most frequent problems in temperament and self-regulation that parents and professionals observe in young children. Read each numbered item and check *No* if the behavior is not a problem. Check *Yes* if the behavior is a problem. Return this form to the individual administering this Screener for scoring and interpretation.

Name of rater: ______________________ Date Screener completed: ____________

Relationship to child: ______________________

	No	Yes
1. Emotions don't match what is going on	☐	☐
2. Gets angry too easily	☐	☐
3. Too easily frustrated	☐	☐
4. Has wild temper tantrums	☐	☐
5. Frequently irritable, "touchy," or fussy	☐	☐
6. Can't comfort self when upset	☐	☐
7. Doesn't pay attention to sights and sounds	☐	☐
8. Seems to look through or past people	☐	☐
9. Resists looking you in the eye	☐	☐
10. Too "grabby," impulsive	☐	☐
11. Moods and wants are too hard to figure out	☐	☐
12. Seems to be in "own world"	☐	☐
13. "Tunes out," loses contact with what is going on	☐	☐
14. Overexcited in crowded places	☐	☐
15. Wanders around without purpose	☐	☐

III. RESULTS

Add all the items marked *Yes*, and place the total in the box below labeled Raw Score. A score of 1or 2 indicates that the child may be at risk for atypical development and self-regulatory behavior. A score of 3 or more indicates that the child's temperament and self-regulatory behavior are probably atypical for his or her age. Follow-up with a complete 55-item TABS Assessment Tool is recommended for any score other than 0.

Raw Score ☐

Recommended for follow-up with TABS Assessment Tool: Yes ❑ No ❑

 ISBN-13: 978-1-55766-423-5 ISBN-10: 1-55766-423-4
Manufactured in the United States of America.

TABS Screener

Temperament and Atypical Behavior Scale

Early Childhood Indicators of Developmental Dysfunction

Stephen J. Bagnato, Ed.D., N.C.S.P. | John T. Neisworth, Ph.D.

John Salvia, D.Ed. | Frances M. Hunt, Ph.D.

Instructions for administering the TABS Screener:

Please refer to Chapter 3 of the **TABS Manual** for important information before administering the TABS Screener. Complete (or have rater complete) the information in Section I. Read and discuss directions for Section II with the rater, making sure that he or she understands how to respond to the items. Ask the rater to return the Screener for scoring and interpretation when he or she has completed Section II.

I. CHILD INFORMATION

Name of child: ______________________________ Sex: Female ❑ Male ❑

Date of birth: ______________________ Age (in years and months): ______________

Child's address: ____

Name of parent or primary caregiver in household: ______________________

Relationship to child: Mother ❑ Father ❑ Other ______________________

Telephone number: ______________________ Best time to contact: ______________

List any previously identified problems or diagnoses for this child.

1. ____
2. ____
3. ____

1-800-638-3775 www.brookespublishing.com

II. TABS INDICATORS

The following 15 items list some of the most frequent problems in temperament and self-regulation that parents and professionals observe in young children. Read each numbered item and check *No* if the behavior is not a problem. Check *Yes* if the behavior is a problem. Return this form to the individual administering this Screener for scoring and interpretation.

Name of rater: ______________________ Date Screener completed: __________

Relationship to child: ______________________________

	No	Yes
1. Emotions don't match what is going on	☐	☐
2. Gets angry too easily	☐	☐
3. Too easily frustrated	☐	☐
4. Has wild temper tantrums	☐	☐
5. Frequently irritable, "touchy," or fussy	☐	☐
6. Can't comfort self when upset	☐	☐
7. Doesn't pay attention to sights and sounds	☐	☐
8. Seems to look through or past people	☐	☐
9. Resists looking you in the eye	☐	☐
10. Too "grabby," impulsive	☐	☐
11. Moods and wants are too hard to figure out	☐	☐
12. Seems to be in "own world"	☐	☐
13. "Tunes out," loses contact with what is going on	☐	☐
14. Overexcited in crowded places	☐	☐
15. Wanders around without purpose	☐	☐

III. RESULTS

Add all the items marked *Yes*, and place the total in the box below labeled Raw Score. A score of 1or 2 indicates that the child may be at risk for atypical development and self-regulatory behavior. A score of 3 or more indicates that the child's temperament and self-regulatory behavior are probably atypical for his or her age. Follow-up with a complete 55-item TABS Assessment Tool is recommended for any score other than 0.

Raw Score ☐

Recommended for follow-up with TABS Assessment Tool: Yes ☐ No ☐

 ISBN-13: 978-1-55766-423-5 ISBN-10: 1-55766-423-4
Manufactured in the United States of America.

TABS Screener

Temperament and Atypical Behavior Scale

Early Childhood Indicators of Developmental Dysfunction

Stephen J. Bagnato, Ed.D., N.C.S.P.
John T. Neisworth, Ph.D.
John Salvia, D.Ed.
Frances M. Hunt, Ph.D.

Instructions for administering the TABS Screener:

Please refer to Chapter 3 of the **TABS Manual** for important information before administering the TABS Screener. Complete (or have rater complete) the information in Section I. Read and discuss directions for Section II with the rater, making sure that he or she understands how to respond to the items. Ask the rater to return the Screener for scoring and interpretation when he or she has completed Section II.

I. CHILD INFORMATION

Name of child: ______________________ Sex: Female ❑ Male ❑

Date of birth: ______________________ Age (in years and months): ______________________

Child's address: ______________________

Name of parent or primary caregiver in household: ______________________

Relationship to child: Mother ❑ Father ❑ Other ______________________

Telephone number: ______________________ Best time to contact: ______________________

List any previously identified problems or diagnoses for this child.

1. ______________________
2. ______________________
3. ______________________

1-800-638-3775 www.brookespublishing.com

II. TABS INDICATORS

The following 15 items list some of the most frequent problems in temperament and self-regulation that parents and professionals observe in young children. Read each numbered item and check *No* if the behavior is not a problem. Check *Yes* if the behavior is a problem. Return this form to the individual administering this Screener for scoring and interpretation.

Name of rater: ______________________ Date Screener completed: ____________

Relationship to child: ______________________________________

	No	Yes
1. Emotions don't match what is going on	☐	☐
2. Gets angry too easily	☐	☐
3. Too easily frustrated	☐	☐
4. Has wild temper tantrums	☐	☐
5. Frequently irritable, "touchy," or fussy	☐	☐
6. Can't comfort self when upset	☐	☐
7. Doesn't pay attention to sights and sounds	☐	☐
8. Seems to look through or past people	☐	☐
9. Resists looking you in the eye	☐	☐
10. Too "grabby," impulsive	☐	☐
11. Moods and wants are too hard to figure out	☐	☐
12. Seems to be in "own world"	☐	☐
13. "Tunes out," loses contact with what is going on	☐	☐
14. Overexcited in crowded places	☐	☐
15. Wanders around without purpose	☐	☐

III. RESULTS

Add all the items marked *Yes*, and place the total in the box below labeled Raw Score. A score of 1or 2 indicates that the child may be at risk for atypical development and self-regulatory behavior. A score of 3 or more indicates that the child's temperament and self-regulatory behavior are probably atypical for his or her age. Follow-up with a complete 55-item TABS Assessment Tool is recommended for any score other than 0.

Raw Score ☐

Recommended for follow-up with TABS Assessment Tool: Yes ☐ No ☐

 ISBN-13: 978-1-55766-423-5 ISBN-10: 1-55766-423-4
Manufactured in the United States of America.

TABS Screener

Temperament and Atypical Behavior Scale

Early Childhood Indicators of Developmental Dysfunction

Stephen J. Bagnato, Ed.D., N.C.S.P.
John T. Neisworth, Ph.D.
John Salvia, D.Ed.
Frances M. Hunt, Ph.D.

Instructions for administering the TABS Screener:

Please refer to Chapter 3 of the **TABS Manual** for important information before administering the TABS Screener. Complete (or have rater complete) the information in Section I. Read and discuss directions for Section II with the rater, making sure that he or she understands how to respond to the items. Ask the rater to return the Screener for scoring and interpretation when he or she has completed Section II.

I. CHILD INFORMATION

Name of child: ______________________ Sex: Female ❑ Male ❑

Date of birth: ______________________ Age (in years and months): ______________

Child's address: ______________________

Name of parent or primary caregiver in household: ______________________

Relationship to child: Mother ❑ Father ❑ Other ______________________

Telephone number: ______________________ Best time to contact: ______________

List any previously identified problems or diagnoses for this child.

1. ______________________
2. ______________________
3. ______________________

1-800-638-3775 www.brookespublishing.com

II. TABS INDICATORS

The following 15 items list some of the most frequent problems in temperament and self-regulation that parents and professionals observe in young children. Read each numbered item and check *No* if the behavior is not a problem. Check *Yes* if the behavior is a problem. Return this form to the individual administering this Screener for scoring and interpretation.

Name of rater: ______________________ Date Screener completed: ____________

Relationship to child: ______________________________________

	No	Yes
1. Emotions don't match what is going on	☐	☐
2. Gets angry too easily	☐	☐
3. Too easily frustrated	☐	☐
4. Has wild temper tantrums	☐	☐
5. Frequently irritable, "touchy," or fussy	☐	☐
6. Can't comfort self when upset	☐	☐
7. Doesn't pay attention to sights and sounds	☐	☐
8. Seems to look through or past people	☐	☐
9. Resists looking you in the eye	☐	☐
10. Too "grabby," impulsive	☐	☐
11. Moods and wants are too hard to figure out	☐	☐
12. Seems to be in "own world"	☐	☐
13. "Tunes out," loses contact with what is going on	☐	☐
14. Overexcited in crowded places	☐	☐
15. Wanders around without purpose	☐	☐

III. RESULTS

Add all the items marked *Yes*, and place the total in the box below labeled Raw Score. A score of 1or 2 indicates that the child may be at risk for atypical development and self-regulatory behavior. A score of 3 or more indicates that the child's temperament and self-regulatory behavior are probably atypical for his or her age. Follow-up with a complete 55-item TABS Assessment Tool is recommended for any score other than 0.

Raw Score ☐

Recommended for follow-up with TABS Assessment Tool: Yes ☐ No ☐

 ISBN-13: 978-1-55766-423-5 ISBN-10: 1-55766-423-4
Manufactured in the United States of America.

TABS Screener

Temperament and Atypical Behavior Scale

Early Childhood Indicators of Developmental Dysfunction

Stephen J. Bagnato, Ed.D., N.C.S.P.

John T. Neisworth, Ph.D.

John Salvia, D.Ed.

Frances M. Hunt, Ph.D.

Instructions for administering the TABS Screener:

Please refer to Chapter 3 of the **TABS Manual** for important information before administering the TABS Screener. Complete (or have rater complete) the information in Section I. Read and discuss directions for Section II with the rater, making sure that he or she understands how to respond to the items. Ask the rater to return the Screener for scoring and interpretation when he or she has completed Section II.

I. CHILD INFORMATION

Name of child: ______________________________ Sex: Female ❑ Male ❑

Date of birth: ______________________ Age (in years and months): ______________

Child's address: ____

Name of parent or primary caregiver in household: ______________________

Relationship to child: Mother ❑ Father ❑ Other ______________________

Telephone number: ______________________ Best time to contact: ______________

List any previously identified problems or diagnoses for this child.

1. ____
2. ____
3. ____

II. TABS INDICATORS

The following 15 items list some of the most frequent problems in temperament and self-regulation that parents and professionals observe in young children. Read each numbered item and check *No* if the behavior is not a problem. Check *Yes* if the behavior is a problem. Return this form to the individual administering this Screener for scoring and interpretation.

Name of rater: ______________________ Date Screener completed: ______________

Relationship to child: ______________________________________

	No	Yes
1. Emotions don't match what is going on	☐	☐
2. Gets angry too easily	☐	☐
3. Too easily frustrated	☐	☐
4. Has wild temper tantrums	☐	☐
5. Frequently irritable, "touchy," or fussy	☐	☐
6. Can't comfort self when upset	☐	☐
7. Doesn't pay attention to sights and sounds	☐	☐
8. Seems to look through or past people	☐	☐
9. Resists looking you in the eye	☐	☐
10. Too "grabby," impulsive	☐	☐
11. Moods and wants are too hard to figure out	☐	☐
12. Seems to be in "own world"	☐	☐
13. "Tunes out," loses contact with what is going on	☐	☐
14. Overexcited in crowded places	☐	☐
15. Wanders around without purpose	☐	☐

III. RESULTS

Add all the items marked *Yes*, and place the total in the box below labeled Raw Score. A score of 1or 2 indicates that the child may be at risk for atypical development and self-regulatory behavior. A score of 3 or more indicates that the child's temperament and self-regulatory behavior are probably atypical for his or her age. Follow-up with a complete 55-item TABS Assessment Tool is recommended for any score other than 0.

Raw Score ☐

Recommended for follow-up with TABS Assessment Tool: Yes ❑ No ❑

 ISBN-13: 978-1-55766-423-5 ISBN-10: 1-55766-423-4
Manufactured in the United States of America.

TABS Screener

Temperament and Atypical Behavior Scale

Early Childhood Indicators of Developmental Dysfunction

Stephen J. Bagnato, Ed.D., N.C.S.P. | John T. Neisworth, Ph.D.
John Salvia, D.Ed. | Frances M. Hunt, Ph.D.

Instructions for administering the TABS Screener:

Please refer to Chapter 3 of the **TABS Manual** for important information before administering the TABS Screener. Complete (or have rater complete) the information in Section I. Read and discuss directions for Section II with the rater, making sure that he or she understands how to respond to the items. Ask the rater to return the Screener for scoring and interpretation when he or she has completed Section II.

I. CHILD INFORMATION

Name of child: ______________________ Sex: Female ❑ Male ❑

Date of birth: ______________________ Age (in years and months): ______________

Child's address: ______________________

Name of parent or primary caregiver in household: ______________________

Relationship to child: Mother ❑ Father ❑ Other ______________________

Telephone number: ______________________ Best time to contact: ______________

List any previously identified problems or diagnoses for this child.

1. ______________________
2. ______________________
3. ______________________

1-800-638-3775 www.brookespublishing.com

II. TABS INDICATORS

The following 15 items list some of the most frequent problems in temperament and self-regulation that parents and professionals observe in young children. Read each numbered item and check *No* if the behavior is not a problem. Check *Yes* if the behavior is a problem. Return this form to the individual administering this Screener for scoring and interpretation.

Name of rater: ______________________ Date Screener completed: ______________

Relationship to child: ______________________________________

	No	Yes
1. Emotions don't match what is going on	☐	☐
2. Gets angry too easily	☐	☐
3. Too easily frustrated	☐	☐
4. Has wild temper tantrums	☐	☐
5. Frequently irritable, "touchy," or fussy	☐	☐
6. Can't comfort self when upset	☐	☐
7. Doesn't pay attention to sights and sounds	☐	☐
8. Seems to look through or past people	☐	☐
9. Resists looking you in the eye	☐	☐
10. Too "grabby," impulsive	☐	☐
11. Moods and wants are too hard to figure out	☐	☐
12. Seems to be in "own world"	☐	☐
13. "Tunes out," loses contact with what is going on	☐	☐
14. Overexcited in crowded places	☐	☐
15. Wanders around without purpose	☐	☐

III. RESULTS

Add all the items marked *Yes*, and place the total in the box below labeled Raw Score. A score of 1or 2 indicates that the child may be at risk for atypical development and self-regulatory behavior. A score of 3 or more indicates that the child's temperament and self-regulatory behavior are probably atypical for his or her age. Follow-up with a complete 55-item TABS Assessment Tool is recommended for any score other than 0.

Raw Score ☐

Recommended for follow-up with TABS Assessment Tool: Yes ☐ No ☐

 ISBN-13: 978-1-55766-423-5 ISBN-10: 1-55766-423-4
Manufactured in the United States of America.

TABS Screener

Temperament and Atypical Behavior Scale

Early Childhood Indicators of Developmental Dysfunction

Stephen J. Bagnato, Ed.D., N.C.S.P. | John T. Neisworth, Ph.D.
John Salvia, D.Ed. | Frances M. Hunt, Ph.D.

Instructions for administering the TABS Screener:

Please refer to Chapter 3 of the **TABS Manual** for important information before administering the TABS Screener. Complete (or have rater complete) the information in Section I. Read and discuss directions for Section II with the rater, making sure that he or she understands how to respond to the items. Ask the rater to return the Screener for scoring and interpretation when he or she has completed Section II.

I. CHILD INFORMATION

Name of child: ______________________ Sex: Female ❑ Male ❑

Date of birth: ______________________ Age (in years and months): ______________

Child's address: ______________________

Name of parent or primary caregiver in household: ______________________

Relationship to child: Mother ❑ Father ❑ Other ______________________

Telephone number: ______________________ Best time to contact: ______________

List any previously identified problems or diagnoses for this child.

1. ______________________
2. ______________________
3. ______________________

II. TABS INDICATORS

The following 15 items list some of the most frequent problems in temperament and self-regulation that parents and professionals observe in young children. Read each numbered item and check *No* if the behavior is not a problem. Check *Yes* if the behavior is a problem. Return this form to the individual administering this Screener for scoring and interpretation.

Name of rater: ______________________ Date Screener completed: ______________

Relationship to child: ______________________________________

	No	Yes
1. Emotions don't match what is going on	☐	☐
2. Gets angry too easily	☐	☐
3. Too easily frustrated	☐	☐
4. Has wild temper tantrums	☐	☐
5. Frequently irritable, "touchy," or fussy	☐	☐
6. Can't comfort self when upset	☐	☐
7. Doesn't pay attention to sights and sounds	☐	☐
8. Seems to look through or past people	☐	☐
9. Resists looking you in the eye	☐	☐
10. Too "grabby," impulsive	☐	☐
11. Moods and wants are too hard to figure out	☐	☐
12. Seems to be in "own world"	☐	☐
13. "Tunes out," loses contact with what is going on	☐	☐
14. Overexcited in crowded places	☐	☐
15. Wanders around without purpose	☐	☐

III. RESULTS

Add all the items marked *Yes*, and place the total in the box below labeled Raw Score. A score of 1or 2 indicates that the child may be at risk for atypical development and self-regulatory behavior. A score of 3 or more indicates that the child's temperament and self-regulatory behavior are probably atypical for his or her age. Follow-up with a complete 55-item TABS Assessment Tool is recommended for any score other than 0.

Raw Score ☐

Recommended for follow-up with TABS Assessment Tool: Yes ☐ No ☐

 ISBN-13: 978-1-55766-423-5 ISBN-10: 1-55766-423-4
Manufactured in the United States of America.

TABS Screener

Temperament and Atypical Behavior Scale

Early Childhood Indicators of Developmental Dysfunction

Stephen J. Bagnato, Ed.D., N.C.S.P. | John T. Neisworth, Ph.D.

John Salvia, D.Ed. | Frances M. Hunt, Ph.D.

Instructions for administering the TABS Screener:

Please refer to Chapter 3 of the **TABS Manual** for important information before administering the TABS Screener. Complete (or have rater complete) the information in Section I. Read and discuss directions for Section II with the rater, making sure that he or she understands how to respond to the items. Ask the rater to return the Screener for scoring and interpretation when he or she has completed Section II.

I. CHILD INFORMATION

Name of child: ______________________ Sex: Female ❑ Male ❑

Date of birth: ______________________ Age (in years and months): ______________

Child's address: ______________________

Name of parent or primary caregiver in household: ______________________

Relationship to child: Mother ❑ Father ❑ Other ______________________

Telephone number: ______________________ Best time to contact: ______________

List any previously identified problems or diagnoses for this child.

1. ______________________
2. ______________________
3. ______________________

1-800-638-3775 www.brookespublishing.com

II. TABS INDICATORS

The following 15 items list some of the most frequent problems in temperament and self-regulation that parents and professionals observe in young children. Read each numbered item and check *No* if the behavior is not a problem. Check *Yes* if the behavior is a problem. Return this form to the individual administering this Screener for scoring and interpretation.

Name of rater: ______________________ Date Screener completed: ____________

Relationship to child: ______________________

	No	Yes
1. Emotions don't match what is going on	☐	☐
2. Gets angry too easily	☐	☐
3. Too easily frustrated	☐	☐
4. Has wild temper tantrums	☐	☐
5. Frequently irritable, "touchy," or fussy	☐	☐
6. Can't comfort self when upset	☐	☐
7. Doesn't pay attention to sights and sounds	☐	☐
8. Seems to look through or past people	☐	☐
9. Resists looking you in the eye	☐	☐
10. Too "grabby," impulsive	☐	☐
11. Moods and wants are too hard to figure out	☐	☐
12. Seems to be in "own world"	☐	☐
13. "Tunes out," loses contact with what is going on	☐	☐
14. Overexcited in crowded places	☐	☐
15. Wanders around without purpose	☐	☐

III. RESULTS

Add all the items marked *Yes*, and place the total in the box below labeled Raw Score. A score of 1or 2 indicates that the child may be at risk for atypical development and self-regulatory behavior. A score of 3 or more indicates that the child's temperament and self-regulatory behavior are probably atypical for his or her age. Follow-up with a complete 55-item TABS Assessment Tool is recommended for any score other than 0.

Raw Score ☐

Recommended for follow-up with TABS Assessment Tool: Yes ☐ No ☐

 ISBN-13: 978-1-55766-423-5 ISBN-10: 1-55766-423-4
Manufactured in the United States of America.